BECOME AN EARTH ANGEL

❧

ADVICE AND WISDOM
FOR FINDING YOUR WINGS
AND LIVING IN SERVICE

BECOME AN
EARTH ANGEL

ADVICE AND WISDOM
FOR FINDING YOUR WINGS
AND LIVING IN SERVICE

SONJA GRACE

f FINDHORN PRESS

Findhorn Press
One Park Street
Rochester, Vermont 05767
www.findhornpress.com

Findhorn Press is a division of Inner Traditions International

ISBN 978-1-84409-645-9

Cataloging-in-Publication Data for this title is available from the British Library

Printed and bound in the United States

Edited by Nicky Leach
Cover design by Richard Crookes
Text design and layout by Damian Keenan
Front cover photograph by Ivan Vicencio

Contents

This book is dedicated to my mother.

As an artist, visionary, and botanist, my mother has laced the threads of my heritage together with fiber, paint, and love. She has traveled the world and immersed herself in cultures, inadvertently learning about her own past lives. My mother's love for history wove the family together like a tapestry. She taught me to paint at a young age and shared the world through art. As a skilled and famous handmade-paper artist, my mother took fiber and created artwork that has been shown around the world. Her numerous lifetimes in Japan are reflected and not forgotten.

But the best part of her life is that she became a self-taught botanist, studying plants, loving plants, and harvesting plants for her paper making. Because of her love for nature I was blessed with a childhood playing in the woods. I owe my understanding of love to my parents, for they demonstrated this to the highest degree. My mother knew this gifted earth angel needed to be grounded to navigate the world. She encouraged me to dance, paint, and create. I am blessed to have the ability to see her for who she is and to celebrate her beauty, creativity, and immense spirit.

Foreword

I remember the first time I heard Sonja over the phone. My heart resonated to the music in her voice and I thought, I am talking to an angel.

Qualities of heaven imbue every nuance of Sonja, an intuitive, healer, teacher, and author. There is a shimmering to the messages and truths she delivers, a purity to her dedication to everything and everyone on this planet—from "two-leggeds" to "four-leggeds" to natural and spiritual beings, visible and invisible.

This celestial tone emanates from every word in her book, *Become an Earth Angel*. Of course, the totality of heaven can't be contained in ink and paper, any more than our physical body can limit our divinity. That's the starting place for the invitation issued by Sonja in this brilliant book—an acknowledgment that the Divine is present in and to us all, assisting us especially through the angels.

As she points out, and as we intuitively know, winged angels transcend all realms. They fly into our nightly dreams, catch us when we're falling, and affirm the most hidden aspects of ourselves. They watch over, guide, and encourage humankind, and always have. But even the most powerful of the heavenly angels now need help—our help. They are seeking individuals willing to be anointed for angelic work, individuals willing to transcend their own fears and inadequate perspectives and operate as angels on Earth—or as "earth angels."

Sonja is an earth angel. She has always been an earth angel, able to perceive and interact with celestial beings. She has also gone a step farther. She has accepted the responsibilities of living as an angel on Earth. She has surrendered her human will to divine will, and actively improves the welfare of all. Because she has made this choice, she is in the perfect position to pose the following question to the rest of us:

Are we willing to accept the duties—and blessings—of being an earth angel?

I embrace Sonja's question with the excitement and sobriety it deserves. Like Sonja—like many of you—I've always been "different." My parents thought me "curious," and not only because I asked a lot of questions; it was because they thought me "odd." As did Sonja, I saw angels as a child. I actually officiated at numerous tea parties with Gabriel, his wingtips constantly knocking over the cups and saucers. I also perceived ghosts, demons, fairies, and shadows of both light and dark. For me, the physical world was a line sketch and all things spiritual were the color—both inside and outside of the lines. Little wonder I would grow up to work as an intuitive consultant and healer, that I would write 20-plus books about spiritual and energetic topics.

Whether or not you perceive the supernatural, the question of becoming an earth angel starts with a request from the heavenly angels. It is they that first notice the potential of a person for "earth angel" status. Under their tutelage and guidance, a person evolves, but only by surrendering—surrendering to this tutelage and guidance. How else can we advance what is most real inside of us all—our angelic nature, our goodness—but by following those who already display these traits?

After all, our human nature is two-fold. In order to transform our lives and the planet, we must be willing to work hard. We must be willing to address our personal karma and practice forgiveness. We must include rather than exclude emotions. We must be ever intuitive but also practical and reasonable. And we must be willing to live authentically, with integrity, selfless giving, and humility.

All this is necessary to become an earth angel, to gain the insight and power necessary to transform our lives and the planet. What an honor, though, to be chosen. What a need, to become the type of person who could be chosen. Indeed, humanity is at a crossroads. If we continue on our current path, we will remain mired in darkness and violence. But we do have another choice. We can embrace the assistance of the heavenly beings and decide to live by the "secret code," the divine code divulged to earth angels, which Sonja explains in her book with a simple word.

I have to tell you one of my own secrets right now. One of the reasons I'm so thrilled to embrace Sonja's work is highly personal. I'm related to her. Yes, one of the fascinating results of our first and subsequent conversations was figuring out that we share the mysterious and hardy blood of Scandinavia, wayward

Vikings most likely included. It is in these frozen denizens that tales are still told of Shining Ones that walk the land and beings with wings that comfort and teach.

Ancestral legends insist that the Scandinavians were a special lot, uniquely blessed by the Divine. (I don't think we're the only ethnicity with ego.) But of course, the angelic visit every land, home, and open-hearted person, as Sonja shares in this deep and warming book. The winged ones are here for us all. The question is, can we say the same?

Can we actually become one, even though our wings might be invisible?

As once declared by Billy Graham: "Look up—take courage. The angels are nearer than you think."

Just think. There might be one in the mirror.

Cyndi Dale

Introduction

There is a new order of earth angels
coming to the fore to help humanity.

My name is Sonja Grace, and I am an earth angel. I have spent my life dedicated to divine love, and for decades I have been called upon to help people in all areas of their lives. There are a small but growing number of people like me walking the planet, who have fully realized their path as an earth angel, but hundreds of thousands of others are beginning to feel the calling of their spiritual light, searching for answers and hoping to discover their path of service. At the same time our planet has moved into the fifth dimension, and we are about to witness the arrival of a new order of earth angels. This book is for those emerging souls who are filled with light and sensitive to an extraordinary degree. It is a guide for the earth angels who are just "finding their wings."

I have always understood there to be something different about me. My earliest memory, at two years old, was seeing figures standing in my room next to my crib. Today, I know they were my guides. I don't remember being afraid of them; I do remember them communicating with me, and I felt a deep sense of peace. I was always referred to as a happy baby, and certainly their presence contributed to my state of being. In fact, they helped me to roll the crib across the floor so it would bang on the door and send my mother running to me—quite a feat considering the crib was heavy and hard to move! I always thought it funny that my mother actually believed I had moved the crib on my own.

My guides are from the angelic realm, and I have worked with them all my life. They assist me on all levels of healing. Angels have never incarnated into physical form, consequently their energy is pure and without karmic threads. Angels are from the Divine, and as benevolent beings they ask for nothing and serve the highest good of the universe.

There are so many kinds of angels it's impossible to count. Of course, there are the archangels, the "superstars" of the angelic kingdom, who most of us are aware of. The archangels have particular roles: Michael clears negative energies, Gabriel clears entities and astral plane energies, Raphael assists in healing, and Uriel clears inappropriate cords, links, or lifelines.

Angels can be called upon at any time, and they are not exclusive to any particular religion. Guardian angels, who are often our family members, are the people in the spirit realm who are in service to those of us still on Earth. They are not "true" angels—like earth angels, they have karma, because they have incarnated before. Earth angels are not a recent phenomenon, as you'll see when you begin reading through the book. Today, they are growing in numbers, particularly as we reach a critical state on planet Earth. We need earth angels more and more.

No doubt you were drawn to pick up this book. It's not an accident. As the book unfolds, you will probably recognize yourself and some common characteristics in many of the descriptions of earth angels. This book is part of my service. I was instructed by my guides to write it and reveal the true nature of the earth angel. Guided by the angels, I am here to lovingly help escort you through your transition.

No one chooses to be an earth angel—you become an earth angel through the initiation of the angelic universe. When my father passed, I helped him to the light as far as I could go before they turned me back. He came to me the next morning, with angels all around him, and touched my head, placing a gold light around the crown. The angels acknowledged my help and told me I had earned my wings. I had turned my life over to God and the Goddess, and now I live each moment with the gratitude and humility of service.

When angels appear to me, they are tall and with wings. The colors cannot be described on a regular palette. The white seems gold, and the gold seems silver, and to me the silver has an energy all of its own. The blues and purples twinkle through what looks to me to be very detailed clothing and wings. The colors change when I view the angels in the different realms. Angels have been depicted in the art world and through visionaries in all shapes, sizes, and colors, but all consistently with wings.

As an earth angel I travel in the angelic universe, never alone but accompanied by the archangels. I feel pressure between my shoulder blades on my back, as if wings are attached. I have felt wings from the angels brushing up next to me, but my flight as an earth angel remains with their assistance. I learned at an early age that there is a different navigational system used when traveling the realms in the universe, and always having a guide or the angels with you is recommended.

The wings of angels are a part of their bodies, and how they move throughout the universe. We always want to compare everything to ourselves, trying to better understand something through the lens of our humanness. Angels are not human, and do not have the experience of the physical form that we incarnate into. Angels have wings so that they can navigate the universe. They are immense beings and have the capacity of transcending all of the realms, being everywhere at once.

Our galaxy has recently moved from the fourth dimension, in which human beings have existed for centuries, into the fifth dimension. It is this shift that heralds the arrival of the new order of earth angels. The best way to describe the dimensions is as energy. As we shift from one dimension to another the vibration is much higher, and in turn our rate of manifestation is super-charged.

The fifth dimension is described in Hopi prophecy as the fifth world. Their belief is that at the end of the fourth world we will see worldwide destruction and division as a result of ideology. Those who do not participate will unite as one race of human beings. In "A Hopi Prophecy" from the *Book of the Hopi*, author Frank Waters says:

You can read this in the earth itself. Plant forms from previous worlds are beginning to spring up as seeds. This could start a new study of botany if people were wise enough to read them. The same kinds of seeds are being planted in the sky as stars. The same kinds of seeds are being planted in our hearts. All these are the same, depending how you look at them. That is what makes the Emergence to the next, Fifth World.

The effect this new fifth dimension is having on sensitive people around the world is profound. You may have experienced dramatic changes or total disruption in your life. Some people have lost their homes, jobs, and relationships and undergone a complete overhaul. Others feel discomfort in their physical body, including a high pitch ringing in the ears. Still more feel lost and have an urgent need to discover why they are here and what their purpose is. The new frequencies on Earth and in our galaxy are reshaping how we experience this world. Our DNA has shifted, along with our sensory systems. While some of this has been painful for many of us, it is necessary, and this process is the key to our understanding. As we test our wings, we must experience our feelings, integrate them, and release. The daily practice of meditation helps the spiritual path become grounded and sets a clear direction for your journey as an earth angel.

The Universe is a complex place, with many aspects unseen and misunderstood. The goal of this book is to help you journey through the different energies of the universe and navigate your own spiritual quest. It is time to step onto your path and realize you are the spiritual being you are seeking. Find your wings and get ready to take flight.

1

Angels Called to Earth

*The energy of angels is at such a high
frequency that they are able to move
through our universe using the realms like
stepping-stones across the Milky Way.*

The concept of angels has been a part of human consciousness as long as we have existed on Earth. These magnifi-
cent beings of light are depicted in ancient art, some wielding
swords and others with gold and silver wings.

A perfect example is *Archangel Michael,* painted by Guido
Reni in 1636, which portrays Archangel Michael trampling
Satan (*http://tinyurl.com/o42k7v4*). The painting currently
hangs in the church of Santa Maria della Concezione in
Rome. A rendition of Archangel Gabriel was painted by an
anonymous artist in the 13th century and now hangs at the
Monastery of St. Catherine in Sinai, Egypt (*http://tinyurl.
com/muorw8d*).

Stories of visitations by angels have crossed all boundaries
of belief. These benevolent beings are called to Earth in many
forms—as archangels, healing angels, and angels of protection—and are experienced in different religious contexts.
The Muslim texts describe the "first revelation" by Archangel

Gabriel to Muhammad in 610 CE. Muhammad is visited by Gabriel, in the Hira cave on the mountain of Jabal an-Nour near Mecca. Gabriel reveals a powerful verse to Muhammad that he is to recite from the Quran. To this day, this episode is as central to the Muslim religion as the angels that appear to the shepherds on the eve of Jesus' birth are to Christian faith.

Of course, angels are found throughout Christian tradition and literature. Joan of Arc is celebrated for the visitations she experienced from several angelic beings. At the age of 12, she claimed divine guidance from Archangel Michael, field commander of the Army of God and the prince of the Heavenly Hosts; St. Margaret, the patron saint of falsely accused people and peasants; and St. Catherine, patron saint of unmarried girls, maidens, and of students. Joan declared that they had told her to help drive out the English from her homeland of France.

The angels reside in the parallel universe that exists in the highest vibration. It is quite literally a vast universe that overseas our universe and is home to Archangels Michael, Gabriel, Uriel, Raphael, and all angels. It is the spirit world we return to when we leave this life. The energy of angels is the closest to Source that we can experience, and is of a high vibration. It has particles of light and substance similar to that of cotton candy: there is substance, but yet there is not—it holds form but disappears quickly. The energy of angels is at such a high frequency that they are able to move through our universe using the realms like stepping stones across the Milky Way.

These benevolent beings are guides related to different realms of consciousness, and they create balance and healing for all who come into contact with them. They instill protection, healing, guidance, and love. Angels are the very essence that protects the Divine. We are all particles of the Divine or God body, and the angels keep an eye on all who enter the earthly realm. The archangels help millions of people around the globe. Many people experience the presence of angels when a loved one is sick or dying, during the birth process, and while engaged in meditation. There is no boundary to where an angel can go; they are assisting us in all levels of consciousness.

We have called upon angels for centuries, and they have answered every time. In certain instances, as mentioned earlier, we are assisted by earth angels, those highly sensitive human beings who share our world but are filled with light and exist at a higher frequency, much like the angels from the parallel universe. These earth angels are rare, and often come from lifetimes of service to the Divine. They are revered as saints, gurus, mystics, and shamans.

St. Winefride, a Welsh woman from the 17th century, was an earth angel who brought healing to the poor and sick and is said to have left behind a sacred healing spring at St. Winefride's Well in Holywell, Flintshire, in Wales. Native Americans revere the life of Lakota medicine man Martin Highbear, who touched the lives of Native Americans from different tribes as well as those of non-Natives. He was an earth angel and is celebrated for bridging the gap between peoples and creating the rainbow bridge.

There are common threads to be found in the lives and work of the earth angels of the past. Many lived in poverty and worked as healers unconditionally motivated by the love of God and the Goddess. They exemplify discipline and integrity in the way they lived their lives.

Earth angel Mahatma Gandhi lived his life for the people. He healed the hearts and minds of his nation through his own sacrifice. His life was spent in service to humanity, and through his spiritual practice he carried a message of peace that is still felt and shared today. Like earth angels before him, Gandhi practiced nonviolence and truth in all situations, advocating that others do the same. He lived modestly in a self-sufficient residential community and wore the traditional Indian dhoti and shawl, woven with yarn hand spun on a charkha. He ate simple vegetarian food, and also undertook long fasts as means of both self-purification and social protest. His efforts to help the people by bringing a message of nonviolence and peace allowed millions of people around the world to shift their own consciousness. The experience of an earth angel involves living life authentically, with humility and respect for all living beings. Gandhi was the embodiment of these qualities as well as compassion and love for his people.

The life of Mother Teresa, a Catholic nun who dedicated her life to caring for the poor, is another recent example of devotion. She was often described as someone with special qualities who had "a love for souls within her," even as a child. She gave up everything to be in service to God, caring for the sick and the dying with unconditional love and compassion only an earth angel offers. On August 17, 1948, she dressed for the first time in the white, blue-bordered sari she was always depicted in. She passed through the gates of her convent to enter the world of the poor and the slums of Calcutta. Mother Teresa visited families, washed the sores of children, cared for an old man lying sick on the road, and nursed a woman dying of hunger and tuberculosis. Each day she proved to the world that we are all divine children of God. As an earth angel, she understood that we are all particles of God and there is no separation. It is believed Mother Teresa was perpetually surrounded by angels and received their assistance daily.

Similarly, Yogananda brought profound healing to people around the world. Like the earth angels before him, he understood his life's purpose at a young age, seeking out many of India's Hindu sages and saints, hoping to find an illuminated teacher to guide him in his spiritual quest. Yogananda met his guru, Swami Yukteswar Giri, in 1910, when he was 17 years old. The awareness of past lives and interconnectedness is evident in Yogananda's relationship with his mentor, Yukteswar. He describes their first meeting as a rekindling of a relationship that had lasted for many lifetimes:

> We entered a oneness of silence; words seemed the rankest superfluities. Eloquence flowed in soundless chant from heart of master to disciple. With an antenna of irrefragable insight I sensed that my guru knew God, and would lead

me to Him. The obscuration of this life disappeared in a fragile dawn of prenatal memories. Dramatic time! Past, present, and future are its cycling scenes. This was not the first sun to find me at these holy feet!

I consider Edgar Cayce, "the father of holistic medicine" or "the sleeping prophet," to have been an earth angel. For 40 years, Cayce gave psychic readings to thousands of seekers, and he became one of the most documented psychics of the 20th century, acknowledged for his deep inner process. He gave many of his readings while in an unconscious state. He diagnosed illnesses, revealed the lives of his subjects lived in the past, and prophesized things yet to come. As with all earth angels, his connection to Source was said to be strong. Cayce used guides and the benevolent beings that surrounded him to help him decipher what he was channeling, because his experience of past, present, and future came to him all at once. Edgar Cayce carved out a place for future earth angels that truly melded the spiritual revolution.

Earth angels often look for a teacher to assist them in their understanding of their work and the evolution of their journey. As I mentioned, it's no coincidence that you were drawn to this book. I have always been in service to the Divine. In many cases, earth angels become dedicated to one particular teacher who provides clarity and understanding for them as they navigate the demands on their unique healing energy.

Part of the journey for any earth angel involves uncovering resistance. The resistance that we all share is the need to confront and parent our inner child. My first teacher was an incredibly loving person but also extremely disciplined. She ultimately brought me to my knees, as she was like a laser, pinpointing where my inner child was ruling me rather than remaining in a car seat at the back of the car! When she sat with her students and went into meditation, it was as if we were in a Tibetan monastery, meditating for hours on end. As a result of her helping me find my way, I dedicated myself to being in service and use the miracle of my gifts to work with the Divine, building upon the solid platform I inherited from her.

The next time I chose to dedicate myself to being in service to others, I was in meditation in my home in Oregon. I traveled through time and space to sit in the center of Mount Shasta, a mountain in California considered a vortex of energies. Sitting with me were the ascended masters, Buddha, St. Germain, Babaji, Yogananda, and Jesus, to name a few, and this is where I learned for the first time that time and space do not exist. Another example occurred a few years later, when I found myself sitting on a hillside in southern Oregon, communicating with Goddess Earth and dedicating my life to being in service to her. Since then, I have dedicated myself many times to being in service, because each time I have done so there has been some profound event that has rocked my world and humbled me.

As the years passed, I continued to recommit myself to being in service to others by means of ongoing ceremonies and vision quests. With each year, with each dedication, I found myself increasing my understanding of what it means to be in service to others and taking on more responsibility. Finally, after years of dedicating myself, I moved into a daily ritual of proclaiming out loud that my life is completely turned over and in service to God and the Goddess. I have now reached a deeper understanding of this lifelong quest and know in my heart that this is my purpose.

Common Characteristics of the Earth Angel

Earth angels share some similar characteristics, which I have listed below. However, as a spiritual teacher and as an earth angel who sees and receives messages from the Divine, I am aware that the process involves your evolution in all areas, including the physical, mental, emotional, and spiritual bodies. Once on your path, it is vital that these characteristics are carefully nurtured and developed in the full understanding of their potential. What follows is drafted from my own experience and from the observations of others:

AUTHENTICITY: Earth angels are authentic. They know who they are and why they are here. They have found their own voice deep within themselves. There is no mask, no façade. There is no investment in the duality.

NEED TO HELP OTHERS: Earth angels share a need to be in service as a way of realizing their earth angel experience. No doubt you too recognize and empathize with the pain of others. Just standing in line in the store, I can "see" and "feel" the energy of others; I "know" what they need. Compassion and love pour from my very being, but at the same time my respect and boundaries for others remain intact, never intruding on someone but sharing my gifts with those who ask.

INTEGRITY: There are many ways to work with energy but the sign of a true earth angel is someone with integrity. When I am called to help others I maintain a space of compassion, no matter how important or trivial the issue. I always ask that my will is aligned with the will of God and the Goddess, and that the work is done for the highest good of everyone and the highest good of the universe. I never use my gifts for gain or power, nor do I allow any pollutants, such as drugs and alcohol, to block my filters. I hold each person's energy with love and respect. I do not converse with any astral beings, such as entities and lower astral plane demons. I only communicate with the angelic realm and with the Divine.

SENSITIVITY: What sets an earth angel apart is that all of their senses, including intuition, are constantly open, and are often felt as an energetic acceleration. Many people experience an opening of one or two of these sensory systems, but it's only the earth angel who experiences all senses at all times. Earth angels experience telepathy, along with vivid dreams and psychic translations of past, present, or future. They experience themselves as constantly in contact with the Divine.

HUMILITY: Humility allows earth angels to transcend the duality, for when they are humble they no longer need to attach themselves to anything. Gandhi lived his life with total humility and showed the world his true strength, his inner peace. The humility that comes from understanding the importance of the earth and all that she gives us is something an earth angel understands. As an earth angel, several times in my life I have experienced sitting on a hillside, praying for four days, with no food or water. This experience has brought the most humility to my life.

HEALING: The gift of healing is something most earth angels are born with. Early signs in childhood show us the past life connection that inevitably brings the healing work to the forefront. The healing aspect is the most difficult for an earth angel, as it requires grounding, awareness, and selflessness. The healer is the one who understands how illness can serve us and helps others to see there is no victimization.

COMPASSION: Like Mother Teresa, earth angels understand there is no soul that gets left behind, for there is no separation between people, cultures, and religion. Compassion is the artist's palette whose colors I work with daily as I encounter so many stories of loss, pain, and hardship across the globe.

SENSE OF PURPOSE: Earth angels know their purpose, for it is deep within them and often discovered at a young age. Each day, I feel a deep sense of purpose. I always pray that my life is in alignment with the will of God and the Goddess, and that my work is for the highest good of everyone and the highest good of the universe.

PAST LIVES: The common thread connecting all earth angels is their experience of past lives as healers, mystics, or visionaries. Earth angels have worked throughout history helping people all over the world. The job of an earth angel is not for the faint of heart; it is for warriors who know where they have been and what they have done.

LOVE: The mission statement for humanity is to love at the deepest level of our beings. The path of the earth angel is one of service, of transcending the duality and embodying such a high vibration of love that there is no seam between this world and the spirit universe. The love I experience in my work is the foundation for all that I do as an earth angel. It is through that experience that I am able to love every person around the world equally, with as much love as I have for my own family.

Have you been called to serve? You might recognize the characteristics of an earth angel in yourself. You are not alone. Feeling a purpose in life is leading thousands to heed the call for a spiritual connection to Source. Prepare yourself as we embark upon the angelic universe.

2

The Angelic Realms

*Angels have never incarnated into physical form,
thus their energy is pure and without karmic threads.
They are of the Divine, and like many benevolent
beings they ask for nothing and serve for the highest
good of the universe.*

I am an earth angel with the ability to travel into the parallel universe. No passport or luggage is needed for this journey. When I enter the universe of angels, I am aware of a bright light that does not have the colors and hues of the light on Earth but a brightness that reaches down into my soul. What follows is a description of my most recent visit to the parallel universe, where angels reside with information passed to me for those emerging souls on Earth.

The parallel universe is as vast and far reaching as our own. The explanation of this universe is not easy. I suggest you stay grounded, with roots like those of a tree going deep into the earth, as together we dive deep into a complex description of my understanding of the realms, dimensions, sectors, and all who live there.

Archangel Uriel appears and asks me to join him. Together, we take flight to the parallel universe where the angels dwell.

I feel wind on my face, and we move up out of Earth's atmosphere. Somewhere beyond where space would be, we merge with an intense bright light that opens into its own infinite space. This is the home of the angels. I am aware we have moved through time and space quickly, yet it felt like slow motion. Here in the angelic world, I find myself moving about as if floating. I'm not walking on anything solid. There appears to be no gravity. But still I move about with ease. My body is weightless. The air seems lighter. The intense light envelopes me, and I experience profound joy and bliss.

I see angels around me—hundreds and hundreds of angels. I am aware of the angels acknowledging my presence. They seem so different here to the ways they have appeared on Earth. To me, they have always revealed themselves as tall and with wings. Their colors are not described on a regular color palette. White seems gold, gold is silver, and this silver has an energy all of its own. Blues and purples twinkle through finely tailored detailed clothing. Each angel's wings are uniquely patterned, transparent, and glistening with extraordinary beauty. The wings are full, with depth and feathers. They are not the feathers of birds but luminescent weavings of gold and silver and, in some lights, white. The weight of these wings appears heavy; they create a wind that could sweep you away but are light and move with ease.

When I see angels on Earth, they have a bright white light around them and their wings glow with gold and silver through the gleaming white. They have strong bodies and appear solid and full of energy. In this parallel universe my vision is without its earthly filters, and in their natural environment the angels are enhanced with prisms of light.

The energy here is pure and without karmic threads. I cannot comprehend the high frequency in which these divine benevolent beings exist. I only know that they ask for nothing, serving the highest good of the universe. As I look around, I am reminded that ultimately our true nature is in spirit form. In fact, all beings in the universe begin and return to this energy. Angels, however, have transcended to such a degree that they can take on a physical shape anywhere in the universe when they need to.

Our human form on Earth is denser and at a lower vibration. There are a growing number of human souls now sensitive to the loving energy I am experiencing here and working hard to raise their frequencies. This may explain why some people "see" or "feel" the presence of angels. They are the open ones, on whose behalf the angels navigate these higher energies and travel the realms, to visit and bring guidance, peace, and love.

I feel light. Love and joy course through every cell, as I turn to look around me and take in this special place. It's truly hard to describe because it's nothing like we have seen on Earth.

Imagine a giant multi-floored, multi-dimensional parking garage, fluid and transparent, with each floor being a vibration or realm. This is the grid our galaxy and universe exist in. It is constantly in motion. Angels are like elevators that can travel throughout the universe, shifting through the various strata of energy and vibration. All galactic travelers move through the realms, which are defined by their particular vibration and energy.

The Realms

The first realm is an underdeveloped space with low-frequency entities, demons, and darkness, which the universe has passed through in various stages of development. Humans also experience this realm when they lower their frequencies to be a match to the energies in the first realm. For example, if we cannot clearly see what we are dealing with in these realms we might mistake something of a lower frequency, such as a demon, for something of a higher frequency. Since humans tend to view everything through the frame of the duality, it's important to take off those particular glasses when feeling your way through the realms in order to stay in balance.

The second realm is filled with disruption, chaos, death, and birth. This is where the earth naturally exists, and where you will find turbulence, such as earthquakes, volcanoes, rivers, oceans, and the natural cycle of life. Humans exist in both the second and third realms. Many have evolved into the third realm. The second realm keeps us connected to a fight-or-flight modality that relates more to the first chakra. For centuries, humanity has existed in the second realm; only recently, has it started to move into the third realm.

In the third realm, we experience more cohesiveness and a willingness to work together. There is communication and a desire to help one another. Humans have joined the Devic kingdom and the animal world in this vibration that connects us with our sense of self. The gateway to the parallel universe exists in the third realm. This means that most living beings will pass through the third realm as they ascend to the light. Think of the realms as though they were different pairs of glasses that alter the way you view what is around you. The third realm is a lot like the third chakra: a freeway of activity with all living beings. We interact with the Devic kingdom and the animal world in this vibration, working together and co-existing.

The fourth realm is a much higher energy, and home to the ascended masters. Buddha, Jesus, Krishna, and many others are in this frequency. The energy in this realm requires an enlightened state of being to handle the frequencies. Any karma that is unresolved will shift the person right back into the third realm. The fourth realm relates to the heart, and through its highly evolved vibration it is used as a gateway by angels to help Earth dwellers. Remember: each floor in the parking garage or realm is a liquid state and constantly moving.

All who are in spirit form can travel through the realms, and each realm has different energy conducive to the needs of different travelers. The most common travelers are the beings that exist naturally in the higher frequencies. Angels are able to travel through all of the realms. The lower entities and less conscious energies can only travel through the first, second, and third realms. The fourth realm is a place to aspire to as we reach for our own transformation. The fourth realm provides a vibration of peace, thereby allowing the experience of the duality as an observation and nothing more. This is quite different to the first three realms, where the duality is the template defining how we experience the realm or vibration we are in.

The fifth realm is a frequency that can be painful if you have not dissolved your karmic threads. This realm is where many beings in the universe naturally exist. Arcturians, Greys, and beings from Sirius are commonly found in this frequency. This energy is foreign to humans and requires a great deal of understanding before venturing into it. Some people experience the presence of aliens, for example. What they don't understand is that the aliens are in a different vibration; aliens don't exist in the same frequency as humans. The temptation with the fifth realm is to put on our explorer's hat and jump in to take a look. I advise extreme caution before attempting to enter the higher realms. Without the necessary structure and support within our own mental, physical, emotional, and spiritual bodies, the consequences could be really dangerous.

The sixth realm is a place where time and space, color and sound all merge into a vibration of light, transforming everything to that frequency. Beings that have never incarnated but have the ability to take physical form are in this realm. The angels use this realm for doctoring and healing. They are able to transform the energy in other realms through this frequency. This is the gateway to the parallel universe that the solar and planetary beings use. They are of such a high frequency they only exist in this realm and higher.

The seventh realm is where the angels naturally exist. This high vibration of white light is infused with a violet and crystalline energy that creates a matrix of light. The angels and their song fill this realm because it is the source of their frequency. They are immersed in the Divine and carry that energy with them, which is why a visit from an angel is always so profound!

As I travel through the realms, Archangel Uriel describes how the energies layer and create the universe. The layers, or auric fields, are much like the layers within your own aura. The earth also has an auric field, with layers defining each energy center. The galaxy and earth exist in one of the many sectors of the universe that radiate outwards from the center. Our galaxy is in a layer that connects us to other parts of the universe. There are so many intricate aspects of our universe to understand. Most remain a part of the unseen, which we tend to dismiss, despite the fact that we feel it. Uriel acknowledges that most of what humans pursue is formed in matter, yet much of these parallel universes are in liquid form, moving and shifting in space until conception and birth.

It is important to understand the different aspects and workings of the universe and how to navigate it as an earth angel. By realms, I mean differing frequencies, particularly the higher and lower frequencies and the energies that resonate there. It helps to understand how we experience our universe through energy. For example, have you ever noticed or experienced people in your life who act as if they still live in the 1800s? These people might carry guns, be abusive to others, or disrespectful of the animal kingdom. I would describe that person as living in the second realm. Their experience is locked into viewing their world through that lens. Another example would be a mother who works, takes her children to school each day, and has a dedicated yoga practice. She is looking at the world and experiencing it through the third realm. If our energy is low and we have a strong victim mentality, we might experience life within the second realm.

Of course, I'm not judging these experiences; I am merely using them as simple explanations of how different some realities can be here on Earth. When I write of the parallel universe, I mean the place where all beings in spirit form live, that is, everything that does not have a body. Realms exist here, too, but they are a gateway for travel for the spirit community. The overall frequency of the parallel universe is the Divine. It is such a high state of love we can't even imagine it. Many scientists believe a parallel universe exists where things are exactly opposite to here on Earth. For example, the oceans are where the land is, but we are all there living life as we are here. I feel the parallel universe is much more than that: it is the spiritual universe to which we all return and where the angels exist.

Uriel leads me to a place where the archangels are gathered. I still move as if I am floating. There is nothing solid to walk on, no gravity; it's as if I am in space. Other angels acknowledge me as I meet Archangel Michael. He tells me that they are happy I'm able to travel into their universe and work with them. He explains why people on Earth need their help and why earth angels are essential and increasing in number. Humanity, he explains, has lost its way; we are disconnected from Source, or God body. Earth angels will help to teach that we must align with Source and take on a great responsibility to care for the planet.

I see my old friend Archangel Raphael. He takes me aside. His energy is warm and protective. We discuss the issue that is so important to me: healing. He explains what needs to be done to help people and how I can continue to call on the healing angels to assist me when I work on people. The healing angels will help instruct and guide not only me but also other earth angels doing similar work. According to Raphael, there is so much heartache and pain on Earth, and the earth angel's job is to help process and deal with that pain.

According to Archangel Raphael, karma is unresolved emotional wounds from past lives that follow us into each incarnation. From time to time, the karma has an exaggerated feeling. The result is a wounded inner child, with both emotional and physical pain that feels like a punishment. Raphael explains how we are souls (a particle of God) in human form, and that in this form we experience the duality. We also have the opportunity to transcend the duality while on Earth. All living things experience pain during their lifetimes.

Ultimately, pain of any kind is about being separated from God. Our connection to God is the ultimate link to our original consciousness, or the translation of the God particle within our soul body. When we are born, we are so overwhelmed with the physical experience we immediately feel a sense of separation from Source. The duality keeps us in a state of separation, as we try to define what is good and bad through the human experience. The angels teach that we can be at a higher vibration, observing the duality but not participating in it—in other words, taking responsibility for our energy.

I see a flash of silver and gold out of the corner of my eye and hear Archangel Gabriel calling me. As he speaks, I feel surrounded by his strength and see him clearly standing in a pool of white light with silver, gold, and indigo dancing around his wings. "As particles of God, humans incarnate into the physical form and pass through many lifetimes," he says. "Whereas, angels are immortals, always caring for the universe, always watching over the earthly plane. Now I want to show you the Devic kingdom and introduce you to Pan. He is the keeper and protector of all plants, trees, and energy of the earth."

The Devic Kingdom Explained

As we travel to meet Pan, Archangel Gabriel talks to me about the Devic kingdom and how the beings of this unseen world are a source of magic on the earth, and that when we, as humans, witness magical beings such as fairies, sprites, or little people, it is proof of the unseen parallel universe. The Devic kingdom is governed by Pan. He is also the caretaker of the energy of the earth and sits at the right hand of the Earth Goddess. The angels work with the Devic kingdom and assist in all they do. They are in charge of the energy field, vortexes, ley lines, and chakras of the planet.

The parallel universe, of which the Devic kingdom is a part, has many levels of consciousness, with angels always working at the highest vibration. Next are the ascended masters, who have incarnated on Earth but transcended all karma. This is followed by the Devic kingdom, which includes the fairies, sprites, little people, and all the plants and the trees. At the next level of consciousness are the animals, then humans, and lastly, the insects. We learn about these different energies in the Devic kingdom because we interact with the earth daily. Earth angels are particularly sensitive to the Devic kingdom.

Archangel Gabriel and I are nearing the Devic kingdom, and as we do he continues to describe how both the angels and Pan fulfill their chief role of caring for the earth and the planetary consciousness. Planets are large beings found in every galaxy in the universe while also residing in the same consciousness as God; they too have souls, which come from the highest vibration. These benevolent beings have incarnated into a much denser physical form, that of a planet, such as Earth, Mars, Venus, Jupiter and the Sun, all embodying a consciousness that far exceeds that of even the angels. They seek to comply with the overall balance of the galaxy and the universe. Protecting Earth and her consciousness is why the angels and Pan's kingdom work together.

Finally, we arrive at our meeting place. Pan's energy melts my heart, cutting to the core. Pan demands truth and is generous with his love for the earth. He appears tall, with the hindquarters, legs, and horns of a goat. His hair is tousled and catches gold light through brown hues. Greek mythology hails him as a god of the wild, fields, groves, glens, and fertility. I see a sparkle in his eyes, as he speaks to me with a generosity and willingness to share.

Pan begins by explaining that God is the source for both universes: the one we reside in and the parallel universe, which religions often refer to as Heaven. Pan describes how the simple task of breathing the air can be overwhelming for humans, even though we take it for granted, because it is filled with *prana*, or energy, and we need to assimilate and transform in each breath. As we breathe, we also exchange energy from our cells with the earth's energy. The earth's energy connects with all living things, and that vibrational exchange is a venue for healing.

Pan tells me to carry a message to all earth angels: We should not isolate ourselves; instead, we should expand our consciousness into nature. When we connect with the trees and plants, we are communicating with a higher form of consciousness. The plant world carries messages in its cellular structure and serves humanity throughout the Devic kingdom. In the past, instead of the cellphones that we now use for communication, we lived close to the earth, and messages were transmitted across the forest with the help of nature. For this reason, I encourage people to go outside and tell the trees who you are and what you feel. They will carry your message all over the land, sharing it with the Devic kingdom. Often, people don't understand this incredible form of communication, because the Devic kingdom has been long forgotten. The trees and plants remember, though, and they will respond to your call.

As their guardian, Pan manages the energy with the help of the Devic kingdom. Incarnations from the Devic world are rare, but occasionally they are granted access to the human form from the Divine. According to Pan, the angels are God's messengers and the only ones who can do the bidding of the Divine. The angels hear our call and come to Earth to help with all areas of the human experience. We are earthbound for a reason: the physical body is very dense and often cannot handle higher frequencies until trained through a spiritual practice. Similarly, we do not leave the planet for a good reason: we are here for the experience of bringing spirit into matter. Entrance to the angelic universe is rarely granted—only a few people are able to gain entrance, with an invitation from the angels. People have been turned away when seeking to enter the bright light where souls travel. Very few earth angels are able to do this, and only because they have been appointed by the angels and can step out of their physical form to be anywhere at any time. This is very advanced, and seldom do earth angels need to enter the parallel universe. They most commonly experience their work within the earth's gravitational field, where they care for the living. The angels are quite particular about which earth angels cross boundaries, and will determine for themselves whether the individual concerned is ready to take such an extraordinary journey.

As the archangels guide me from the parallel universe through the realms and different vibrations back to this earthly plane, I realize how honored I am to have experienced so much with their help. My meeting with Pan in the Devic kingdom has made me more determined than ever to share with new earth angels the message that we need to be more sensitive to the needs of our environment and every living creature dependent on the earth.

As earth angels, we are constantly guided by the angels and reminded, almost on a daily basis that we are never alone! Consequently, it is vital that we keep our bond strong and our connection open. Below is one of the centering processes I use to connect with the angels.

Connecting to the Angels

Close your eyes and feel your breath deep in your belly. Ground your energy into the earth, like roots from a tree going deep into the ground. When you are making your prayer, ask for the angels to help you and assist with that prayer. Ask that your will be in alignment with the will of God and the Goddess. Ask for the angels to guide you and protect you and that their light always surround you, your family, community, and the world. Thank them for their help and guidance.

3

Archangels

*This is a time for all humans to take
responsibility for what we have created and
collectively work on healing not only our self
but the planet, too.*

Angels exist in a vibration that allows them to come to
Earth and materialize. People recount stories of benevolent encounters with angels who appear to help them and then
disappear once the situation is resolved. Michael, Gabriel, Raphael, and Uriel are the archangels, and they often appear to
help those who ask. I often call upon them for assistance, but I
know they will also go to the aid of people who never think to
ask for their help. What follows are descriptions of each of the
archangels as I have experienced them in my role as an earth
angel.

Archangel Michael

Archangel Michael is the leader among the archangels. His
name means "He who is like God." He has been adopted as
the patron angel of the police, firefighters, soldiers, protectors
of truth, surfers, dancers, car racers, wrestlers, bodybuilders,
football and basketball players, sun and beach worshippers,

and sports players. Michael's main purpose is to rid the earth of negative energies. His own energy is fiery, and when he is near, people have reported seeing flashes or sparkles of bright blue or purple light. People call on him for protection, strength, courage, direction, energy, life's purpose, motivation, clearing spaces, clearing entities, and self-esteem.

Michael is larger than a human and moves through the ethers at lightning speed. He has dark hair that falls to his shoulders. He wears an iridescent blue, silver, and gold robe and carries a sword. He is a warrior and uses his sword to release us from fear within the duality. When Michael is present, I feel his wings envelop the space we share and command the energy in the room. There is warmth and a violet light. I often call on him to clear negative energy since part of his job is to oversee and balance the elements of positivity and negativity in the duality. Michael is the bridge to Earth for many people seeking help in turbulent times. When calling upon Michael, allow your mind to clear and ask him to help. Often he carries a violet flame, which clears negativity using the powerful energy from the angelic realm. His gold-glimmered clothing turns to armor if the negativity he encounters is powerful.

Archangel Gabriel

Archangel Gabriel is the messenger angel. His name means "God is my strength." He is the archangel of action and communication. Gabriel helps those involved in the arts or communication by creating opportunities for others to express their talents. Gabriel has been adopted as the patron angel of writers, speakers, philosophers, actors, poets, physicists, computer geeks, bloggers, entrepreneurs, life coaches, and motivational speakers.

Depictions of Gabriel often show him with a lantern in his right hand and a mirror of green jasper in his left. The mirror represents the wisdom of God as a hidden mystery. His entire being emits a bright white light that permeates the space. Gabriel will often arrive in someone's life when they become conscious of the need to communicate and deliver an important message to our world. Gabriel helps them to fulfill their life's purpose of "spreading the word." He might also appear to you when you are ready for a new beginning or a new direction in life, because it is Gabriel's mission to reveal to you the truth of your purpose. Gabriel awakens the inner angel that is aligned with the higher self, reminding us that true liberation is achieved through the divine order of the universe.

Deeply compassionate and motivated by a love for humanity, Gabriel is considered a fierce warrior who assists with clearing entities and astral plane energies. Entities are from the astral plane, which is a space that exists between this universe and the parallel universe. Everything, from the highest angels to the lowest entities, exists in the astral plane. Entities are dark energy forms that have shape but not a lot of density and become attached to people because there is an opening in their energy field. Demons also exist in the astral plane, as well as aliens who travel without form.

I never speak to any of these lower vibrational energies, but call on Gabriel to help clear them. I call upon Gabriel because his light dissolves these beings and transforms them into a higher frequency. The lower energies want to move into a higher frequency, which is why they attach themselves to human or pets. Some inhabit the human form, causing behavioral changes in that person. Pets will also take these on to protect their owners and act out with behavior that is not normal for them. When I am clearing entities, demons, or aliens, I will ask for all of the archangels, depending on how severe the situation is. I recommend for the uninitiated earth angel to not attempt to "clear" anything they cannot see. This is also true of spirits who have passed and helping people with their journey back to the light.

When we leave it up to the angels, the best is done for all involved. I see Gabriel offering comfort to those who have lost loved ones, as he guides individuals who are passing into the light. He is there to help souls transition into the light. I have seen Gabriel put his wings around those who need to be helped to the light, moving them swiftly into that parallel universe.

Gabriel is the oldest of the archangels, followed by Michael, Raphael, and Uriel. They were created by God and evolved in a time and space with no beginning or end. Of the winged angels, Gabriel was the first. As I mentioned earlier, he is also the most responsible to the spirit world, in charge of guiding other forms of life back to the light. When the earth was created, the angels governed a whole different race of extremely intelligent beings from another part of the Universe. Some of that energy remains on the planet today, and as we discover more evidence of ancient beings here, it reminds us that there is so much more to this consciousness called God than we realize. Gabriel says it is God that creates all life forms and manifests within each one of them.

Archangel Raphael

Archangel Raphael is a healer of physical bodies, both for humans and animals. His name means "God heals." Those who call on Raphael are healed rapidly, and he can be invoked on behalf of others. Raphael will go where he is requested but cannot interfere with a person's free will. Archangel Raphael assists with clearing inappropriate cords, links, or lifelines.

Raphael has been adopted as the patron angel of astronomers, doctors, nurses, healers, herbalists, intuitive, travelers, light-workers, therapists, shamans, and medicine women. He helps with eliminating addictions and cravings, clairvoyance, eyesight, support for healers, retrieving lost pets, clearing spaces, releasing spirits, and protecting travelers.

Raphael is often depicted with his right hand leading the biblical figure Tobit and holding a physician's alabaster jar in his left hand. The apocryphal book of Tobit tells the story of angelic intercession and the healing powers of Archangel Raphael. He is the physician of the angelic realm, and helps all earth angels find the love, compassion, and the beauty in service to the healing of others. He gently guides us to harmony, including healing all of our relationships, past, present, and future. His energy is peaceful, and he possesses the power to cast out demons.

From time to time, I may call upon Raphael to help me with the physical energetic surgeries I carry out on clients or to help me work with clients who have diseased organs or tissue. Raphael is the embodiment of healing and often uses sound or music frequencies to work through dense physical matter. Music is a healing therapy, and it has been shown to engage the entire brain. It is no surprise that music is so important to us all.

When Raphael is called upon, the healing is received through sound vibration and music. However, his music is of such a high frequency that it is impossible for mortals to hear it on Earth. The sound vibrations are deep and powerful and pierce through the ailments in ways we cannot comprehend. Interestingly, unusual sounds or high-pitched frequencies are being heard more often around the world, and this is transforming the DNA in humans, plants, and animals. Raphael is helping us shift into these higher frequencies, as part of a transformation to the fifth dimension.

Every one of the archangels is responsible for life on Earth, as well as in the parallel universe. Though he is not called upon as often as Gabriel and Michael, Raphael's compassion, love, and nurturing of all living things is unsurpassed. He is the leader of a host of angels doctoring the sick, wounded, and suffering around the world. Raphael takes care of us physically, and also helps to mend and repair souls crossing over through death. He can help with the healing of cancers, loss of limbs, heart attacks, and more.

Archangel Uriel

Archangel Uriel is one of the wisest archangels and is often seen leading the way. His name means "God is Light" or "Fire of God." He gives prophetic information and warnings and illuminates situations. He has been credited with bringing the knowledge and practice of alchemy to mankind. He is regularly depicted holding a sword in his right hand and a flame in his left. Archangel Uriel assists in clearing links, which are chords or connections with others that exist in this lifetime but are past life related.

Archangel Uriel brings emotional harmony and mental clarity to those who feel lost, abandoned, rejected, or alone. He has been adopted as the patron angel of judges, lawmakers, peacemakers, and seekers of truth, prophets, and visionaries. He can be called upon to help with alchemy, divine magic, Earth changes, solving problems, students and tests, the weather, and writing. Uriel is also involved in deeply serious matters and helps scholars and prophets. I think of him as the old sage, the one to call on for creative insight and intellectual information. Uriel is also helpful to us mortals during earthquakes, floods, fires, hurricanes, tornadoes, and natural disasters. In fact, he can change these events, or help us recover in the aftermath. Like Archangel Michael, Uriel protects those who call upon him by transmuting negativity into the light.

Help From the Angels

The current transition into the fifth dimension has many people on edge here on Earth. Some people are experiencing heightened emotions and finding it difficult to stay grounded, while others are developing physical symptoms, such as cancers, illnesses, and degenerative diseases. The drastic weather patterns, from severe cold to excess heat, that we've been experiencing are also mirrored as changes in our bodies, too.

Of course, the good news is that there are many angels here to help us maintain a spiritual state of mind. The angelic realm has saved humanity many times through the ages, and once again, as we face a multitude of changes that will affect the human race for millions of years to come, they are with us. We must all do our part. The message from the archangels is clear. Begin by taking action in your heart and become a caretaker of the planet by sending your loving energy into her body, heal yourself and help the planet by tending your inner garden. Be mindful of your thoughts and focus on love.

The angels understand our fears about the future. They encourage us to love the frustrations and disappointments, because in the long run, the only thing that really matters is how much you loved and how much you shared your love. This is a time for all humans to take responsibility for what we have created and collectively work on healing not only ourselves but the planet, too. Remember: you are already the inner galactic traveler and spiritual being that you seek; now let every step you take be your connection to the Divine.

Meditation for Inner Alignment

I am a divine child of the universe, and I deserve to be here as a soul in a body on the earth. I deserve to be loved, cherished, and cared for, abundant, happy, healthy, and filled with joy. I turn over all of my worries and fears to God and the Goddess, for they are better off being managed by the Divine. Now that I am free, I will celebrate being alive and feel my feelings, process them and release them every day! I will cherish each moment and ask the Divine to help me to accept the things I cannot change, the courage to change the things I can, and the wisdom to know the difference.

4

The Fifth Dimension

*There is no greater power
than divine love.*

The human race has come so far in its development. In just the past 200 years, we've witnessed the industrial age, breakthroughs in technology, and now we're moving swiftly into the robotic era. Life on Earth has shifted many times, and we get to glimpse only a tiny sliver of her history during our own existence. Advances in medicine and science have changed the length of our lives, and saved even more. The seven billion-strong residents of this planet now have electricity, running water systems, public education, and new areas of scientific studies, all of which are changing the very structure of our society.

We have leaped through the past one hundred years, breaking new ground in technology, far surpassing what astronomers and visionaries dreamed of in the past. Poverty does not wear the face of a world community anymore. Although there are still extreme food shortages in war-torn and drought-ravaged areas, there have been tremendous strides in the fight against world hunger.

Earth Karma

As we enjoy the comforts of the modern world we have created, we must also remember the issues that we as humans continue to battle against—issues such as pollution, disease, and war. These are the problems that the new wave of earth angels has been called upon to assist in solving. For example, according to the World Health Organization (WHO), more than 3.4 million people currently die each year from water-related disease, yet there are more people on Earth with mobile phones than a plumbed and flushing toilet. They also estimate that instances of cancer could reach 24 million a year by 2035, if we don't change our ways.

But most worrisome for the angels—and in turn, earth angels—is the potentially devastating issue of climate change. This beautiful planet, of which we are the caretakers, is in danger: the temperature is rising, ice is melting, and sea levels and water temperatures are changing. The oceans are the biggest contributors to climate because of their vastness, so changes in ocean temperatures in turn impact the saline content of the water and the other interconnected elements that control sea life. Impact on the weather patterns is already being felt—the geostrophic wind patterns have shifted due to changes in ocean temperature, and consequently, we are experiencing stronger storms and fluctuating temperatures. Rainfall levels are being impacted around the world, and according to Dr. Kieran O' Mahony at the University of Washington, the planet is undergoing a radical shift to adjust to these new series of events.

In my opinion, the energy of the fifth dimension is responsible for bringing about climate change and the reshaping of the earth's land and oceans in order to match the new frequencies of this dimension. The old energy is being expelled from the earth, and so too are centuries of war over religion, land, water, airspace, and natural resources. In the past, these issues have been a source of collective karma, which created an ancient thread that wove humanity together. Today, we must realize that we are not bound to living in the past but to creating the future. As earth angels, we must heed the call to do something and become more active by responding to that inner voice, the same one that has directed you here. I see this time on Earth as critical and realize that many people will leave the planet due to the intensity of the fifth dimension.

I believe that as earth angels, we must work together to ensure a future for our children and the many generations to follow, and that means protecting our planet. Mother Earth provides for us unconditionally—after all, it is she who brings us to life. Mother Earth's evolution is similar to ours, but her larger body means her life is extended beyond ours and she also has a connection to the deities that rule the stars.

One might think that the earth has karma in the same we do, but actually that is not the case. The earth is a benevolent being that does not incur karma; her whole existence is about maintaining a state of balance. The earth does not experience the duality in the way we do, because her frequency is similar to the angels. She does not look at us through the lens of right or wrong; rather, she is intent on keeping things in balance.

Even though her "body" is vast, she works to keep it in balance; for example, she might let off some steam in Indonesia with a volcanic eruption or similarly shift her tectonic plates in California, but it's all in an effort to maintain her equilibrium. She feels better, just as you do when you can shift your body back to a comfortable position.

Along with the threat of climate change we face other dangers in the fifth dimension, and as earth angels we need to remain attentive at all times. In particular, we must be vigilant when it comes to the pursuit and application of scientific knowledge. Just like Oppenheimer's breakthrough in atomic energy brought both positive and negative consequences, the work of the scientists at the Large Hadron Collider on the border of Switzerland and France has the potential to do the same. The experiments taking place inside the largest particle divider ever built and the search for the God particle has the potential to teach us so much. But we know so little about these experiments. The physicists are planning to attempt to recreate the Big Bang through a massive underground explosion that could be too much for our fragile earth to handle. There are many scientists who have protested these experiments and only a handful who understand what is going on.

It is important to protect our global health and be aware of what mankind is creating and how quickly it can change our reality. The fifth dimension calls all earth angels to be aware, helpful, and prepared. We are the ones tasked to take care of others during the transformation of this new energy, which is changing us at the very core.

The Fifth Dimension:
What It Is and What It Means
to the Earth Angel

Regular science does not acknowledge the existence of a fifth dimension. In the hardcore factual world of science, there are only three dimensions of space: up/down, left/right, and forward/back. There is a fourth temporal dimension—that of time. However, things in the scientific world are changing, which comes as no surprise to earth angels. Recently, scientists have begun to discuss and investigate the notion of a fifth dimension, and even a six, seventh, eighth, ninth, and tenth dimension. It's complicated science, and too involved to go into here, but the very fact that scientists are using "super-string theory" and experimenting with particle physics (such as the work being done at the Large Hadron Collider) indicates it's only a matter of time before proof of our multi-dimensional world is discovered.

Earth angels understand the fifth dimension in this way: it is the energy in which we currently exist. It is found in the air, the sky, and the rays of light defining our space. The fifth dimension is the same vibration as the fifth chakra, with a high frequency and connectivity through the electromagnetic field among all living things. The color frequency is indigo, with a sound tone of E flat, which makes us increasingly telepathic and acutely aware of the space between this world and the spirit universe.

For all souls on Earth, the fifth dimension is like living in your fifth chakra! This means that sound is clearer and more defined, the sense of smell is heightened, and our ability to hear is more acute. In some cases we can "hear" another person's voice without them speaking. Light looks different, and colors often appear to be layered with a shimmer that can be seen in the sunlight. The fifth dimension redefines communication by bringing truth to the fore, particularly about topics that have gone unspoken, such as government, aliens, and secret societies.

Earth Angels and the Fifth Dimension

The frequency of the fifth dimension is allowing a growing number of souls to become aware of their spiritual path. Seekers from all corners of the world have spent lifetimes preparing for this new vibration. Earth angels are taking the lead, helping to shift the consciousness of humanity. The fifth dimension heralds the end of humanity's continuing incarnation on this planet, and the earth angels are helping with this transition from one soul group to the next. In fact, as the fifth dimension progresses and strengthens, new souls will come to Earth from different parts of the universe. They are star beings, here to continue the cycle that has existed forever: incarnate, experience, remember, and move on.

My introduction to the fifth dimension started in the mountains of Oregon, when I was sitting deep in meditation and completely detached from time and space. The angels took me to the center of the universe, and I witnessed a milky-white energy, which they told me to step into. As I merged with this energy, I felt such a physical sensation of bliss I was smiling and weeping at the same time. This was not the euphoria one feels in meditation; this was the entire physical body engaged in bliss. I was there for some time, and when I came back it was actually hours later. I was transformed that day, knowing that this is the energy we are meant to experience while in physical form, and that the fifth dimension is key to people having a more direct experience of Source.

Earth angels will understand the need to help others integrate the energy of Source into their lives. Some earth angels weave the Divine into their daily practice, helping people around the world. Donna Eden is a profound energy healer who works with the meridians, chakras, and the aura, balancing the systems for optimum health. She pioneered energy medicine. Cyndi Dale, who is an energy healer and intuitive coach, has spanned the globe with her incredible angelic being. She has also brought energy medicine to the forefront, helping people to recognize their own abilities as earth angels. Barbara Brennan is a scientist who understands the human experience through energy and vibration and has helped people heal around the world. Margaret Ann Huston is an earth angel who sings her way through life, healing with sound and energy—her songs are as healing as her hands. Many more earth angels contribute daily and prepare the new earth angels for their mission here on Earth.

In fact, the field of conscious health and healing is growing exponentially, with gifted practitioners emerging every day. It is no surprise that the market for healthy living, sustainability, and all things mind, body, and spirit is over 2 billion dollars.

There are many more earth angels contributing daily and preparing for new missions here on Earth.

Exploring the Fifth Dimension

Looking back on previous dimensions helps our understanding of this one. The third dimension ended before the time of Atlantis and Lemuria, around 21,000 BC. During the third dimension, people were concerned with power and dominance over food sources and water. It was tribal living, survival of the fittest, and the human experience was denser and more combative. The energy was similar to that of the third chakra.

As the fourth dimension drew near, humans struggled to overcome their need for power through war and domination. Toward the end of the third dimension, a greater energy became available through the heart and reflected a need for love and compassion. Some tried to live from the heart, while many others feared letting go of power and dominance. This resulted in centuries of hardship, through wars and stories of monumental love and sacrifice.

English history reminds us of Anne Boleyn, one of the six wives of Henry VIII, who was an example of power and love that nearly collapsed relations between England and the Vatican, as well as France. The display of power and the experience of love shook England to the core. Anne Boleyn was beheaded in 1536 and remains to this day one of the most famous queens in English history. The human race experienced hundreds of lifetimes in the fourth dimension, discovering "the heart": feeling love, losing love, being devastated by love, and leaving love. There was enormous emotional pain, but it was a necessary part of understanding and growing in this frequency. Some people went deep into their hearts, speaking, sharing, and in some cases dying for peace as part of their greater love for the human race as a whole. We are reminded of a great earth angel, Martin Luther King, Jr., who led the Civil Rights movement and was killed in 1968, leaving the hearts of many people around the world grief stricken. This example of love transcending power and resulting in peace is the higher octave of the fourth dimension.

The experience of the fourth dimension remains part of us, even though we have moved into the fifth dimension. We brought the experience of love along but left the trials and tribulations that come as a part of loving behind us. In the fifth dimension, we are called to be present, to communicate truthfully, as well as be responsible for our energy and the survival of the planet. Some people will drag their feet, as with all transitions. What we record in the karmic history book during this fifth dimension will be important to the entire human race; this is not a time for self-indulgence. Remember: we are here as the caretakers of the planet. Mother Earth simply witnesses our journey but has no karmic tie to the species she grants shelter to. She is without karma and gives of herself freely.

The Fifth Dimension and the Physical Body

The fifth dimension affects the four essential bodies: the physical, the emotional, the mental, and the spiritual. The frequency of the fifth dimension is integrated into the physical body of humans through their exposure to charged particles from the sun and the galaxy, found in solar flares, coronal mass ejections, coronal holes, filaments, gamma ray bursts, and galactic cosmic rays. These charged particles affect and gradually transform human DNA. In fact, vibrations from the sun and cosmic rays from our galaxy affect the electromagnetic fields of all life forms in the fifth dimension, including planets, asteroids, comets, stars, and galaxies. The cosmic rays also act as a form of communication between the galactic bodies and the solar system.

The higher frequency of the fifth dimension also creates shifts in time and space. Some people experience time shifts in their everyday lives, such as arriving at their destination considerably earlier than they had expected and without remembering the process of getting there. This is not because they were speeding or daydreaming; this is because they are allowing the energy of the future to meet them before they have arrived. In the fifth dimension, the future is like a liquid energy forming as we send out a signal to create a solid conjunction of energy. As we visualize our arrival point, we find ourselves almost feeling teleported to the destination because we have clearly connected with the future. This must be observed within the context of our karma and life purpose. We might visualize what we want for the future, allowing that vision to form in the liquid energy, but with the understanding that our karma and life purpose also create a vibration that influences what we manifest in the future.

Our ability to manifest has increased in this fifth dimension. We are more tuned in to the intention we set when we are designing our future. Our intention is very important, along with not being attached to what we want to create. The paradox in life is to be in it and to be detached from it. We want to manifest what we want, and our minds are clear that this is right, but the earth angel knows that there is no attachment to anything, only observation and compassion. When we look at this future and align with the formation of what is to come, it is helpful to remember that although we might feel powerful here on Earth, we are mere mortals; it is always best to let God and the Goddess create the future, based on what we hold in our hearts. When we find ourselves out of alignment, or dealing with energetic emotional components stored in the body, we must also pay attention to what is manifesting in this new frequency.

The energy of the fifth dimension increases the pain we feel in our bodies from minor aches and pains to more severe illnesses, such as cancer and autoimmune diseases. These illnesses often manifest as a result of unresolved emotional wounds from this life and our past lives. I call those holdover emotional issues from past lives "karmic threads," and they must be addressed and healed if we are to function in this higher frequency. Both individually and collectively. we will discover that the fifth dimension prevents us from lingering in the past or from holding on to previous sorrow or pain. Many people fear and avoid processing emotional hurt, but in the fifth dimension it is a mistake to ignore emotional pain, because it will be taken on physically in the form of illness.

Imagine the human body is like a car, given to us on incarnation, so that our soul might experience being here on

Earth. Much like a favorite car, it is our job to care for it. The body is home to our original consciousness, which contains the God particle and provides the higher frequency for the physical body to integrate with the Divine. As we raise the frequencies of the physical body we can better manage the experiences on Earth. Meditation, yoga, and sound create a practice that allows all of the essential bodies—the physical, mental, emotional, and spiritual—to come together as one.

Meditation helps us to integrate these new energies from space, or downloads from the Original Consciousness. Meditation creates the best conditions and opportunity for grounding, assimilating, and experiencing the higher frequencies, the realms, and the angels. Allowing our bodies to feel the emotional process helps us to understand how it is the physical that becomes the warehouse for our feelings. The fifth dimension demands that we process these feelings and release them. Later on in the book, I will offer a selection of meditations.

The Fifth Dimension and the Emotional Body

I view the emotional body as our homework. In the fifth dimension, humans have the responsibility to process and release their emotions, and as earth angels, we are called to assist people in this process. Emotion carries energy. Just think about the energy that comes off someone who is feeling sad or happy; we tend to pick up on those signals. We translate experience through feelings, and grounding those experiences is vital to our emotional and in turn physical health. "Trapped" emotion creates karma, the unresolved emotional wounds from past lives. Karma resides in the physical body through the energy centers called chakras. If emotion is untended, then illness and disease are the result. All illness is a derivative of the emotional body.

Collective karma is an emotional response to events shared with thousands of others. This also needs to be resolved as a soul group. Endless fighting, hating, criticizing, and jealousy result in collective karma for all humanity. For example, we have experienced collective karma in the form of war since the beginning of the human experience. World War II took millions of people back into the collective pain of shock and betrayal. We have witnessed episodes of genocide in many cultures, and our energy goes out to those who are affected. Unfortunately, however, when we engage our energy sympathetically we can hook our energy up into that event, thereby keeping the cycle alive and creating more karma for the collective. When we ground our energy, it helps us to avoid dialing in to the collective karma.

How We Got Here

How we got here by way of our family of origin is important to understand. When we are born, we choose parents with whom we have karma. They are our soul pod, and we often go back lifetimes with these souls, changing roles and genders with each incarnation. Each incarnation is an opportunity to work through the emotional scars of previous ones. We may switch "soul" families over the centuries, and with each incarnation we will find ourselves in a lifetime with those with whom we have the most to resolve.

Karmic threads connect us through lifetimes of experiences. Sometimes, we feel like we have met someone before or have been to a place that feels familiar, even though we have never traveled there. This would be an example of a karmic thread.

Our past lives are an important part of our experience. They are the history of the soul's journey as it works through the karma incurred over lifetimes. I believe we have incarnated not only on Earth but on other planets, too. In my experience, few humans remember past lives or understand the reason for their existence, but the higher frequencies of the fifth dimension mean that we must look beyond this life to release and process deep-seated negative emotion.

When I read past lives for clients, I am able to see all the way back to their first incarnation on Earth. When I connect with a person's past lives, I start with where they were born, and I literally follow the path of their soul up to the parallel universe and back down to where they were previously. Each lifetime, I travel back, following the soul up into the ethers and back down to Earth, being shown the entire life like a hologram in my office.

For example, a female client had a phone session with me and explained that she was under suspicion from her siblings who believed she was trying to steal from them what was her rightful inheritance. I looked into her past lives and found out that she had a lifetime in England in the 1500s. She was accused of being a heretic and burned at the stake. I then discovered another lifetime, in the 1400s in France, where she was again female. This time she was accused of adultery and imprisoned. She became sick and froze to death in prison because of the poor conditions. She was born a male in yet another lifetime, in 1200 CE Rome. This time, she became entangled in a web of deceit and was accused of stealing. Once again, she was put to death.

What we uncovered through these past lives was a pattern of being wrongfully accused, betrayed, and abandoned. Finally, we went back to the beginning of these patterns and karmic threads and discovered that she had been a female in the Mayan culture and as a child taken from her family to be sacrificed. It was this horrific experience from which all the patterns stemmed. I cleared the fear and shock that had cemented the karma to my client's life. Months later she came back to me to tell me that the veil of suspicion had been lifted and she and her siblings had settled their differences over the inheritance. Understanding your karma and clearing the past, forgiving those who push your buttons, is the fast track to healing.

We have had centuries to address and handle our karma in order to be ready for this new energy in the fifth dimension, but unfortunately, so many of us have not done the work. Remember: part of what we were being called to do in the fourth dimension was the inner work. During the fourth dimension the heart was activated, leading us to heal; some took that path, while others got lost in the experience. Many people recognize this now and are working hard to resolve old wounds and heal from within what is now the fifth dimension.

This exemplifies the importance of the earth angel's role in healing. First, we must address our personal karmic history and then help others to address theirs. Earth angels put themselves at risk psychologically if they work on others without working on their own personal issues first. The practice of forgiveness is key—both forgiving others and forgiving ourselves. Sometimes it feels impossible to forgive someone. I remember a particular client of mine whose daughter was murdered. While it's important to hold someone accountable for what they have done, we must find it in our heart to forgive them, no matter how difficult, so that the karma doesn't recur lifetime after lifetime. In this particular case, the father, the daughter, and the murderer all shared karma—specifically, they were part of a karmic triangle. I was able to help clear their karma and release the old threads to the past.

In order to do work like this, though, I have had to work diligently on myself and my own karma, each and every day. Earth angels work best from a platform of peace. Archangel Michael warns that withholding emotion is a misuse of being a soul in a body. Earth angels are to be immediate with our emotional experience, feeling our feelings and processing and releasing them, otherwise there is no unity in the physical, mental, emotional, and spiritual bodies. Remember: all that exists in the spirit universe is love, and all beings there are immersed in the highest vibration of love. While this vibration, the highest vibration, is incomprehensible to humans, ultimately, the more we experience our feelings, the more we connect with the energy that can help in our healing and well-being.

The Fifth Dimension
and the Mental Body

The mental body is what we know best. Intellect is celebrated in society, and many of us prefer the challenge of absorbing and understanding information than paying attention to our emotions. The mental process often negates emotions and other sensory systems built into the body. As I explained earlier, each dimension requires different aspects of brain function.

In the fifth dimension, the new sound frequencies are stimulating the mental and bringing new information to the fore. It is fundamentally an energetic process, which is translated through the vibrations of the higher frequencies that are now coming to Earth. Sound can both stimulate and heal the mind by invoking emotion, which in turn helps to release stress chemicals and lay down new neural pathways in the brain. There are many people who have high levels of sensitivity to sound. For some sound sensitivity is actually painful and unbearable—for example, those people who are on the autism spectrum, or those with selective sound sensitivity syndrome, and many others with tinnitus. However, there are an increasing number of people who can hear these extraordinary new frequencies, and in some cases, these new sound frequencies are also linked to our telepathic abilities. I will explain more about that later on in this chapter.

Another challenging aspect of the fifth dimension is the need to balance the mind and heart rather than rely solely on the intellect, which was the requirement of the old paradigm.

Earth angels are here to teach us to move toward our emotion rather than away from our feelings. Of course, as we continue to learn, achieving that balance is not always easy. As an earth angel, I make sure my energy is going deep into the earth; grounding while staying in my heart helps me to filter and process what the mind is receiving. Usually, we connect to the duality through the mind: it is here that we traditionally assess what is right and what is wrong. But surprisingly, as we learn to balance the mind and the heart we learn to trust our feelings, almost like an inner compass pointing the way.

Without balance we resort to processing the duality through the mind only, and in turn we doubt our instincts. This inner compass has a direct connection to our original consciousness—what we call that "deep inner knowing." The truth, as we know, ultimately comes from Source. Once again, I recommend a regular meditation practice to help access, distinguish, and understand the insights available at the physical, mental, emotional, and spiritual levels.

The fifth dimension is about finding a healthy equilibrium between the mind and heart, letting our intellect and emotional intelligence inform one another, as opposed to what we were doing in the fourth dimension, which was rich in pure emotional experience. During the sixth and seventh dimensions, which are literally light years away, our existence will be more about the mind becoming the focus for processing information and experiencing life beyond a dualistic world.

The Fifth Dimension
and the Spiritual Body

The spiritual body is our energetic connection to Source. The karmic record of each journey through differing lifetimes is stored in the soul. The spiritual body has shape and form, just like the actual body we inhabit. The soul is housed inside the energy of the spiritual body, and life fills the skin and eyes with a source of light from within. The angels connect to the spiritual body. They are there when we incarnate and there when we die and return to the parallel universe. Intuition, extrasensory perceptions, and angel communication are experienced through the spiritual, and as I mentioned earlier, the telepathic abilities of human beings are heightened in the fifth dimension. Telepathy works through the spiritual, and we may receive messages from friends or family members in this way. Telepathy is the psychic communication between people. We receive a message from another person through the mind and simply know what is being communicated: for example, the voice of your guardian angel telling you to wait. We receive these messages daily.

We've all had what we might call telepathic experiences. You may find yourself thinking about a friend, pick up the phone to call them, and find that they are on the line. It is no coincidence! This is about the actual event of telepathy. The thought you had and sent out to your friend is telepathy. My Native American heritage connects me to my life on the Hopi Reservation, where I experience the people communicating telepathically all the time. My grandmother knows when something has happened, not just because of her own intuition but because of the connectivity among family members. This is true around the world, in all cultures.

Many indigenous people have a connection within their tribe, which behaves almost like an inner clock. They "know" when activities or ceremonies are about to begin because they share group energy, one state of mind, or a telepathic connection. One-mindedness can be extremely powerful, especially when a group thinks or prays for the same thing, such as water, fertility, or health. These things are often the focus of tribal ceremonies. Telepathy is dialed in automatically because they live closer to the earth and share the same focus. When we are living close to the earth, we are connecting with a source of energy that is imperative to our human experience. Tribes that work in unison with the land, water, air, and sun naturally connect to the earth's energy, but many modern-day humans who don't experience living in a natural environment find themselves out of tune with the earth. Fertility and crops are the bases of any culture, but those who live with the land, dependent upon what they grow and the water source available to them, are going to be more connected telepathically, for they are of one mind with a single goal.

As we navigate the higher frequencies of the fifth dimension, we may all begin to experience telepathic incidents more often. You may find yourself talking to a friend in your mind, and they relay this information not realizing how they came to know what they know. This is telepathy, and the more we ground our energy, connect with the earth's energy, and trust that our message is being heard, the more we will experience a higher level of communication.

Once again, meditation helps to attune these skills. When we learn to quiet the mind, slow our breathing, and expand the belly, ribcage, and lungs, we can start to move into a deeper state that allows us to connect with the Divine. According to Archangel Michael, our spiritual bodies are a vibration that, like a note played on the piano, sends a signal that matches up with that vibration in the universe. It is your God particle communicating with the Divine—sort of like the pinging of a satellite with a signal here on Earth.

This connection is the true nature of our spiritual bodies. We all have a particle of God within our soul that is the beacon of light each human carries. We are connected through this particle, and yet our expression is individual. Individuals express their individuality through their personality, life purpose, individual karma, and psychology. Some earth angels might express their individuality through different healing modalities. There are many ways to express our connection to the Divine. Allow your individuality to shine.

The Spiritual Body and the Hara

The spiritual body is also home to the *hara*, which according to many metaphysical teachers, means "sea of energy." The hara is found at the navel, about two inches below the skin, behind what those in the Hindu tradition call the second chakra, or second center of spiritual power in the body. The hara is important to the energy of the fifth dimension, as it is the portal to higher frequencies. If we sit in meditation and experience our focus through the hara, we can achieve a better understanding of the fifth dimension.

My experience of the hara is profound. When I go and sit in deep meditation I "see" the energy field and understand why the Taoists view the hara as a divine portal into the etheric energy, which surrounds the whole planet. The awareness of the hara and this energy is critical for earth angels because, during meditation, it helps us to separate from our mind and access those higher vibrations available through the portal. Here's another way to look at it: the *chi*, or energy of our body, is centered at the hara. The Taoists refer to it as "the cauldron," because it is here that all the energies of the body meet and are then redistributed throughout the body. When the hara is open, the energies of the body and the etheric energies mix through the portal and help us to maintain good health and vitality.

The Secret Code

The Greek philosopher Plato, like Pythagoras before him, believed the secrets to the universe lay in numbers and in math and that there is order and logic to the universe. Academics and mathematicians from as far back as the time of Babylonia have pursued a secret code. Coded language, such as hieroglyphics created by the ancient Egyptians, was also believed to contain the secrets of the universe. In 196 BC, the Rosetta Stone was engraved and recorded events surrounding the Egyptian King Ptolemy V Epiphanes. The British physician and physicist Thomas Young deciphered the engraving while looking for secret codes. He discovered three writing systems, which led to an understanding of all Egyptian hieroglyphics and revealed a highly developed society of sun worshippers, but it did not reveal the secrets to the universe. We know the Egyptians also revered astronomy and aligned their pyramids to the stars. Scientists and historians have looked at these alignments and searched for patterns and hidden messages in them. In addition to astronomy, the Egyptians also valued astrology and numerology, which use math as a vehicle to unlocking the mysteries of the universe. But to date, no one code has been discovered or deciphered.

Interestingly, though, as we have moved into the fifth dimension, new discoveries are coming to the fore. One British academic, in particular, Dr. Jay Kennedy, has recently discovered sequencing, codes, and symbols in Plato's academic writing that are based on the Greek harmonic musical scale of 12. Plato believed Pythagoras's earlier assumptions that the alignment of the stars and the planets make an inaudible but harmonious sound—a frequency undetectable to the human ear, which is precisely what I have been describing in the earlier part of this chapter. Dr. Kennedy believes it will take generations to really unlock the secrets of the symbols hidden in the texts left behind by Plato, but he could be on to something. Who knows? Perhaps deciphering the messages left behind by one of the greatest minds to ever walk the planet could unlock the real secrets of the universe.

But for me and other earth angels on the planet, there really is only one source, one single code to which everything can be reduced. It is the universal code of love. There are many ways to achieve the understanding and knowledge of the universe, but the experience and connection to divine love truly is all we need. When we die and leave this world, love is the ticket to Source, the original consciousness and the parallel universe to which we return. There is no greater power than divine love. Love washes all other energies null and void. Love is the gateway to Source. Through the spiritual body we can connect with divine love and align our experience on Earth to our purpose. All earth angels need to understand this at their core—identify your abilities, create a pathway of service, and trust you have unlocked the secret code. In this frequency, we can also recognize that what matters is not *what* you do but *how* you have turned your life over to Source in order to serve the highest good of everyone and the highest good of the universe. The secret code is your experience with the Divine. Love at the deepest level of your being and you will have the wings to carry out all of the work that is ahead of you.

During the fifth dimension, earth angels will discover that attachments to the material and physical world will only continue to create karma and prevent the earth angel from serving at the highest levels. There is no room for egocentric behavior, only selfless giving, humility, and service to humanity and the earth. A life in service to each other and to the earth will help to regenerate our planet and the celestial bodies around us. Living in the fifth dimension means moving, thinking, and intuiting at a higher vibration. It also gives the earth angel access to the secret code of the universe.

5

The Divine Connection

*Our Source is very complex, with many facets
of energy, light, creativity, productivity,
and originality all woven together with love.*

We are all a particle of the Divine, and it is important that, as an earth angel, we learn how to care for and maintain this benevolent connection, no matter where we are or what we are doing. The direct line to Source keeps the soul ignited and filled with life. For an earth angel, it is like having a direct conversation with God, day and night, so we need to work at keeping the connection clear and prevent the filters from being compromised. A daily ritual of prayer and meditation is the best way to keep our connection open and attuned to the higher frequencies. Later on in this chapter, I will suggest some ways in which to do that.

I like to think of our connection to the Divine as a kind of spiritual telephone line—a way to talk to God and get answers to our questions and to share our concerns and our gratitude. Unfortunately, many people have little understanding of their relationship with the Divine, and they are either disconnected completely or struggle to maintain a healthy and open relationship with God.

As an earth angel, I have seen many people who have little or no connection to God whatsoever. Emotional hurt or trauma experienced before the age of five creates psychological wounds, and without some attempt to deal with those scars, the individual experiences separation from God. For those who have never experienced any kind of spiritual relationship, there are such deep wounds from childhood that it is as if a door has been closed. Different levels of denial are expressed through drugs, alcohol, work, shopping, sex, and abuse, to name but a few. Some people who live in a deep state of denial end up experiencing a trauma that can often crack the door open. For others, separation from Source creates a feeling of deep despair, leading to abandonment and depression in adulthood. Maintaining our divine connection involves emotional work to heal the inner child.

Becoming an earth angel requires keeping the line to God open. Earth angels, for the most part, have done the work and bared their souls; their readiness to work with others has been acknowledged by the angelic realm, and they have implicitly agreed to keep doing their own emotional work. Going deep into our emotional body and surrendering the ego is a road traveled by few of us, but it's essential in order to work effectively as an earth angel. Helping others means you have first helped yourself.

Earth angels need to take the time to pray and meditate in order to maintain that deeper understanding of the infinite source we are all connected to. Preparing ourselves for a daily union with God and the Goddess allows us to maintain a much higher frequency, which helps us as we do our work. I suggest daily prayer and meditation, including the ritual of clearing the energy field before beginning.

Before I take time in my day to meditate or pray, I clear the energy field, or aura, around me. Native Americans use the sacred cedar plant to eradicate negative energies from the body and from the home. I use cedar daily to clear my auric field, to clear between each client (even though they are on the phone with me), and to clear my home in the same way. I have a heavy bowl or conch shell in which I burn the cedar. I light it, let it flare up, and then blow it out, using the resulting smoke to clear around my body, the room, and around the house. I say a prayer and thank the spirit of the cedar and acknowledge the help I am receiving. If you are sensitive to smoke, or are in a place where you cannot burn cedar, then use the violet flame. The violet flame is an energy that often accompanies Archangel Michael. You can ask for the violet flame in your meditation or prayer to cleanse yourself and your space.

The aura, or large space around you, is like a microphone to the Divine. When we clear the aura, we maintain our energy at a higher frequency and we address the seven layers of the auric field that relate to the chakras. The fifth dimension creates a pathway from the fifth chakra that goes right out of the mouth, engaging the voice and allowing an expression of what we learned in the fourth dimension. Love is the fourth chakra and what we learned in the fourth dimension. This energy rises from your heart and is expressed through your voice.

BECOME AN EARTH ANGEL

As I have discussed previously, sound is an integral part of the way the energy of the fifth dimension is expressed. For the earth angel, the voice is a vehicle for this new energy. Sound also helps to keep the auric field clear.

Sympathy Versus Empathy

An earth angel needs to know the difference between sympathy and empathy. This is important for anyone in service, for sympathy can debilitate the light worker, healer, doctor, or nurse, but empathy helps us to stay in our hearts. Sympathy emanates from the second chakra. People around the world experience sympathetic feelings daily, investing their energy into a situation, lending their feelings and care to others, all the while creating more karma for themselves and the collective. When we are empathetic we come from the heart, which is the gateway to Source. Divine energy descends through the top of the head. At the heart, it meets the energy from the earth, which rises from the bottoms of the feet. When we are in a high state of love, we can handle anything. Earth angels can better help others by staying in the heart and filtering what comes at them through empathy.

Prayer

The first question to ask when creating a prayer is: What is your prayer about? What you are asking for? The most important aspect of the prayer is the vibration surrounding its creation. By moving into your heart and feeling the prayer from a place of love you begin to create a vibrational match with the Divine.

If you are praying for healing from illness, I suggest you love your disease. Most people want to reject what afflicts them and be repulsed by what is in their body. The more we reject what is happening, the more separation we create. This goes back to what I have said about emotional wounds from childhood creating a feeling of separation from God. Illness or disease in the body is also an expression of being out of sync with some emotional aspect within. I believe that if we surround the illness, the pain, and the cells with love we can heal much faster. I also recommend to clients that they get a picture of a healthy organ, spine, or brain and put it up on the wall so that they can love that picture and visualize that healthy state inside their own body.

Let your prayer be one of gratitude. Thank God and the Goddess for the good health you have and for the healing you are receiving. Approach all of your needs and wants with gratitude for what you have. Fear is often felt in the first or second chakras of the body, so as you pray send love to the place where you feel the fear.

Sit and be quiet. Close your eyes and allow your mind to be still. Let go of the thoughts in your mind. Find the "voice" of your heart by dropping your consciousness into your chest. This voice is clear and void of the criticism that can go on in the mind. If you find yourself jumping ahead and running lists of things you have to do, you are in your mind. If you analyze what you are doing or criticize yourself, you are in the mind. The voice of the heart is patient, kind, and forgiving. Your prayer can be sent through this voice in the following way, allowing the mind to be at peace:

> Thank you God/Goddess for providing me with good health in my body, mind, and soul. I love feeling good and have healthy cells. I am grateful for the healing that takes place every day in my physical, mental, emotional, and spiritual bodies. Thank you for keeping me safe. I am grateful for my life.

In this prayer we have surrendered to the Divine and accepted that God is a better director, producer, and choreographer of our lives than we are. We merely need to acknowledge the future as if it is this moment.

Desperation, Fear, and Prayer

Debt and unemployment commonly lead to fear and desperation. The feelings trigger old patterns and emotional wounds from childhood that are linked to our personal karma. Finding gratitude in the middle of an emotional cycle can be difficult. But creating a prayer that builds a connection to the earth provides a space for the Goddess to step in, ease our worries, and make a safe place to let those feelings surface.

A great way to do this is to go outside and literally connect with the earth. Mother Earth hears your pain and sorrow. Tell her your story. Share what is going on and release the anger, upset, and fear to the earth. Allow your feelings to go into the ground. As our mother, she expects us to share all aspects of our lives.

Thank you, Creator, for my life and all that you provide for me. I am grateful for the food I have and the job that awaits me. My energy is now aligned with the future. I surrender my resistance and attachment to the past, including those who have wronged me. In gratitude, I thank you for always providing for me. I love my home, family, children, pets, paying the bills, driving the car, buying groceries, and good health. I ask that my will be in alignment with the will of God/Goddess, for the highest good of everyone and the highest good of the Universe.

This prayer is a good example of how we can align our energy with the Divine. We can acknowledge what we have, even if there is only one slice of bread left. It is important in the fifth dimension to create prayers as if you are in the future, acknowledging what is yet to come while staying in the present moment. Our energy goes out to the universe like fireworks on the Fourth of July. The universe is reading our signal like the Sunday paper! As an earth angel, I find myself in prayer for many people around the world, and no doubt you will, too. Be in a state of gratitude, so that you are creating a balanced future for all who look to you for guidance.

Letting go of expectation is another aspect of prayer that the earth angel needs to incorporate into their work, whether praying for themselves or on behalf of others. Ultimately, we are not in charge of the way things turn out. When we say a prayer to the Divine, it is always in accordance with the will of the Divine and for the highest good of everyone and the highest good of the universe. This way we are prevented from engaging in what we want. When our will gets involved, the vertical power current that exists in all of us becomes compromised.

According to my research, the vertical power current runs through the center of the body, all the way up to God, and all the way down to the center of the earth. The chakras hook into this power chord, drawing in and releasing energy. In her book *Light Emerging*, healer, therapist, and scientist Barbara Ann Brennan says that the vertical power current is "a large channel of energy into which all the chakras release the energy they take in from the universal life or health field all around us. The energy emanating from all the chakras laces up and down through the vertical power current. Each color is woven together, somewhat like a rope made of beautiful, pulsating light of all colors."

The chakras and their relationship to the layers of the auric field are important to understand. Each energy center is inserted like a tubular flower into the vertical power current at its specific location. The chakras spin fast clockwise and keep our organs and physical body healthy. The vertical power current holds divine energy that not only generates life through our chakras but also provides the structure we need to handle being human.

Meditation with the Divine

Meditation quiets the mind and focuses breathing. It can take a great deal of practice and discipline to learn how to meditate, but once you get the hang of it, it is like riding a bike. There is no stopping your ability to expand into nothingness. There are many benefits to meditation, but for the earth angel one of the most important benefits is learning how to ground our energy and recognize where our energy is going, being mindful not to invest in the duality. The aspiring earth angel begins to recognize their energy and where they are investing it, along with the power of observation.

For me, one of the best meditation practices is one that involves the hara. You may remember that in Chapter Four, we discussed how the hara supports the aura and connects us through its portal with the etheric energy. It is also the place in the physical body where intention is set and held. As Barbara Ann Brennan points out, basically, your hara "corresponds to your deeper spiritual purpose." The discipline of sitting in meditation helps the earth angel to overcome the hectic pace, high stress, and demands of regular life on Earth—those things that create pressure, overwork, and feelings of exhaustion, un-happiness, impatience, and frustration. These are precisely the aspects of life on Earth that prevent earth angels from operat-ing effectively. Below is my signature grounding meditation. You may find that taking 15 minutes a day in focused medita-tion actually creates more time in your day.

Sonja Grace's Signature Grounding Meditation

Close your eyes and allow your breathing to slow, as you take air in through your nose and out through your nose, with the tongue resting gently on the roof of the mouth. If this is uncomfortable, then breathe in whatever way is best for you. Drop your consciousness into the first chakra and feel the floor or chair beneath you. Create a cone of energy from the first chakra, with the smaller opening of the cone at the chakra and the wide base going all the way down to the center of the earth. Never send your chakra anywhere; you are simply creating a cone of energy that goes all the way down to the center of the earth in order to ground it.

Now go into your belly, the second chakra, and create a cone of energy that goes over the first cone all the way down, deeper and deeper, to the center of the earth, and ground it.

Feel your consciousness in your solar plexus, or the third chakra, and imagine it like a clear, calm lake. Create a third cone of energy that goes over the first two cones, watching it go down, deeper and deeper, further and further, to the center of the earth, and ground it. Feel the tremendous base you have with the first three chakras grounded!

Now go into your heart, or fourth chakra, and let it be like a three-dimensional sun with rays of love shining out toward others and rays of love shining in toward you. Create a cone of energy from the fourth chakra and see it going down inside the first three cones, all the way to the center of the earth.

Take your consciousness into your fifth chakra and feel your throat, soft and supple. Create a cone of energy, and feel it traveling down inside the heart cone, deeper and deeper, further and further, to the center of the earth, and ground it.

Go into your sixth chakra, and let your mind be clear, as if you are looking at a blank movie screen. Create a cone of energy that goes inside the other cones, letting it travel deeper and deeper, further and further, to the center of the earth, and ground it.

Move into the seventh chakra or the top of your head, and allow it to open like a flower, blossoming open. Create a cone of energy that goes inside all the other cones, and ground it deep into the earth.

Acknowledge your higher self and God and the Goddess. Ask that everything you do be in accordance with the will of God for the highest good of everyone and the highest good of the universe. Ask for the violet flame to transmute any negative energy, any negative thought forms, up into light and love. Ask Source for the white light, the golden light, and the blue light to descend and fill every cell in your body.

This grounding meditation allows you to ground your energy, as well as receive energy from the earth. The earth's energy charges our energy systems throughout the physical body. When we use this grounding meditation, we can connect cones of energy deep into the earth and align with the Divine. When our energy is grounded, we are able to help others and recognize we do not have to engage our energy into the situation to be helpful. Earth angels can establish clear boundaries using this meditation. During every moment of our existence, we emit energy through our words and actions. The energy creates the aura, which is like an internet connection, only in this case directly linked to Source and on continually, even when we sleep. This energy is like a signal going out from our body into the universe. That signal is "read," or deciphered by the Divine, and signals are sent back to us. Consequently, if we are conscious of our energy, and mindful of it through meditation, we become responsible for the kinds of "messages" we are putting out into the universe, and can take care to emit only the kind of energy that has a positive impact on the world and the greater cosmos. This is why prayer is so helpful, because when we pray and are mindful of our intent, we construct conscious and heartfelt thoughts and remain in a state of balance.

It is often said that we reap what we sow, and what we put out there into the universe will come back. If we are grumpy, angry, or bullying, these energies will manifest daily in our lives. If instead, we are compassionate, loving, and kind, these energies will be the vibrational match we experience. The Divine is simply here to support your experience as a soul in a body on the earth. There is no punishment from God, only the intention of creating balance. This is the duality experience here on Earth. Rather than being immersed in one side or other of the duality, it is better to be a witness in a position of observation. That way, you will not emit signals or energy pertaining to either good or bad; you will be a beacon of peace and balance, because that is your internal experience.

Balance really is the objective, especially in respect to the duality. In choosing to only notice one side of the duality, we are actually creating an opening for the opposing side to strengthen. By declaring that we're only going to express positive energy, we tip the scales and the opposite energy becomes stronger somewhere else in the world. For example, some people in the spiritual revolution express the need for only living in "the light" and having positive thoughts. What they don't understand is that this means they are fully participating in the duality, and while it was never their intention they have created separation. Somewhere else in the cosmos, negativity is in full force—it all becomes a balancing act between good and bad, light and dark. If, however, we recognize the duality for what it is—a template for experiencing life on Earth—and step back and observe it, rather than be in it, we will understand what the Tibetan monks have been up to for centuries! They understand the duality is not real; it is an illusion in the earthbound experience.

There is one more important aspect to the duality that I need to explain: the Four Places of Consciousness.

The duality contains two distinctive parts. One side is feeling right, positive, light, and good; and the other side, is feeling wrong, bad, dark, and negative. Those two positions are often polarized between people and countries. This is why, at the turn of the millennium, we still witness war and violence, even while many people feel they are well on their way to enlightenment. The third position is that of observation, as I explained above, and the fourth position is what observation leads to: peace. Peace is derived through a strict practice of deep meditation, which allows you to not only observe but also arrive in a completely new state of consciousness. There are no words to describe the peace I feel when I am in or out of meditation.

Earth angels often ask how to feel their feelings, process them, and release them in a dualistic environment. Well, it's a good question, and the answer is that earth angels are encouraged to feel, process, and release; but rather than invest in the drama of a situation, they should watch it and recognize they no longer want to spend their energy creating signals to the universe that could lead to more lifetimes of karma. The balance we are striving for is found in that place of observation where true peace resides. When we can learn to ground our energy, we discover what the illusion really is.

Ceremony, Rituals, and the Earth Angel

Ritual and ceremony are among the most useful tools in the earth angel's tool kit. I use personal rituals to enhance my day and keep myself present and connected and use more formal ceremonies and rituals when working with clients.

My morning ritual involves always greeting the sun and the earth and thanking them for the beautiful day ahead of me. Even if it is raining and cold, I am in gratitude. I make everything I do a connection to the Divine. My breakfast is made with a prayer, as I offer some of my food to the spirits. I try to experience many aspects of my life ceremoniously—pouring a cup of tea, taking a bath, or driving to the store.

In some cases, I am asked to perform more formal ceremonies as part of my work as an earth angel. Examples of such formal ceremonies might include blessing a child or a woman with fertility. I am often asked to set the energy for days of meditation or create a "safe" space when working with clients. I usually begin, as I explained earlier, by burning cedar to clear the aura and space for the ceremony. I always like to acknowledge the elements: the water that gives us life, the air we breathe, the earth we walk on, and the fire that keeps us warm and heats the food we eat. I may even begin the ceremony with prayer. Depending on the reason for the ceremony, I might create a circle of the participants, symbolic of the cycle of life.

One of the most important things I do in any ritual is to ask that my will be in alignment with the will of God and the Goddess, for the highest good of everyone and the highest good of the universe. Of course, as an earth angel, I make sure that I acknowledge the angels and ask for their help with the ceremony. It's important to stay grounded and state the intention to both the earth and God. Finally I make sure to release my desire for any outcome.

As a part of the Native American culture, I am deeply respectful of and private about rituals and ceremonies I have learned. I am well aware that it can actually be dangerous to try to copy any of the tribal ceremonies that I or others may have witnessed, especially because most people do not understand the medicines and preparations that go into them. In many tribes, there are several people involved in putting on a ceremony, with separate people carrying a part of the sacred knowledge. Never does one individual control all of the knowledge. If something is not passed down through the family line, then the ceremony is no longer performed.

The safest option for any earth angel when they perform any formal ceremony is to make sure that they create something that is not taken directly from another culture but designed from their own hearts.

On my father's side of the family, I hail from Norway and was steeped in Norwegian culture during my childhood, including the gods of Norwegian myth: Odin, Thor, and Freyja. During my youth, I experienced a profound connection to the Devic kingdom, which carried me deep into the woods as I prepared my senses for an even greater awareness. The trees spoke to me and the fairies kept me company while I wandered through the forest. My Norwegian ancestors came through to me and whispered stories about fairies, elves, and the nine worlds connecting the organic experience I was having in the woods to an ancient ash tree called Yggdrasil. It was my Norwegian ancestors who led me to the trees, where I communicated with the Devic kingdom.

As an adult, I found incredible parallels between Native American creation stories and the old Norse myths. These influenced and guided me to ceremonies that would change the course of my life. Both cultures believe in nine worlds and the tree of life.

As part of my Native American background, I sat on a hillside under the watchful eye of a medicine man and prayed for my life for four days without food or water. This type of Native American vision quest is not done without guidance and requires great preparation. The importance of following such instructions is ever present in Native culture but often overlooked by others. I tell my students about how this vision quest taught me to appreciate the bare bones of being alive—essentials like food and water, which unless you have fasted with only prayer and connection to the Divine to sustain you is hard to understand. We learn to appreciate the glass of water served in the restaurant more than ever before. The water in your shower or bath becomes sacred. I pray over the water I use daily in gratitude for the water spirit and for the healing my body receives.

Ceremony is an important part of what holds any culture together and in both my Native American background and my Norwegian heritage there is one common link: food. Whenever my Norwegian grandmother cooked we had traditional food from Norway, and she made sure that we understood that the most vital ingredient in any of her recipes was love.

When I spend time on the reservation, it is mostly spent in the kitchen, preparing traditional dishes, and I often find myself preparing poultices for healing. I have learned how to prepare traditional Hopi foods with the appropriate intention, commitment, and seriousness required and how to serve them the Hopi way. Despite all the seriousness, there is always plenty of laughter and playfulness in anticipation of the ceremony. But food preparation is a serious business.

For example, when I first married my husband his paternal grandmother was not ready to accept me. My biggest problem in her mind was that I did not know how to make "traditional" donuts in the way she preferred. I remember standing on the doorstep of her home at the village with tears streaming down my face because she was not happy with me and she did not hold back in telling me so. My husband and I got in the car, and I decided to declare out loud that it was a good day to make donuts! We drove to our home an hour away, and I prepared dough, completely winging it without a cookbook. Of course, the angels were right with me in my kitchen. I had called upon them because I knew that getting this donut thing down was crucial for my future with my husband and his family. I believe that that day I made a platter of donuts that rivaled any from the grocery store!

Later that afternoon, we got back in the car and drove to my husband's grandmother's doorstep. Platter in hand I presented my donuts, tears streaming down my face. She smiled, shocked at my arrival with the donuts. But she didn't miss a beat—she looked at them and then accused me of buying them from the store! I cried out in protest and said that I had made them. She took them and smiled, and from that day forward always invited me in with a big hug.

What I have learned from both cultures is that ceremonies bring us all together. We share our bonds and commonality, and we find our strength in each other. Ceremony is more powerful when we operate as a group with one mind and one heart. I believe we gain a lot when we pray alone or ritualize events, but we are stronger when we are together.

My life on the reservation is a constant reminder of how little people understand the rhythm of the earth and how my tribe struggles to keep that connection. They battle poverty, drugs, and alcohol, all the while keeping their ceremonies intact. There is no running water or bathroom facility in many of the houses. I am again humbled by my surroundings and grateful I have a house with running water.

Opening a Ceremony or Ritual

An earth angel goes beyond all religions, all cultural beliefs, and embraces everyone in the same way. Our responsibility to the Divine is that we have no expectation but that we truly surrender all that is and live in the present moment. Earth angels find themselves choosing to live a different kind of life—a life that is more conscious of what they are putting into their bodies and how they are managing their filtering system for each energy center. So approaching a ritual or ceremony is important for the earth angel. We must lead from what we feel first. Allow the ceremony or ritual to be simple.

Some people like to use props, such as crystals and stones. I suggest you keep the energy clear and only use what is appropriate for the occasion. Crystals are powerful and often misused. The earth has them deep inside her body for a purpose! We continue to harvest crystals without considering what this element means to our planet. I feel that there is more power in a crystal that has been buried in the yard or by a favorite tree than in one that has been sitting in your house. Rocks are also powerful, and those of us who have a habit of picking them up must remember they carry a powerful energy. Rocks that come from the ocean are linked to that vibration and will pull energy wherever they are placed. River rocks are also filled with the energy of water and can set things off kilter if not placed outside where they naturally connect with the ground. In other cases, when a person is sleeping and they are not feeling grounded at night, placing a rock by all four legs of the bed frame will ground that energy. People wear stones and crystals to shift their energy and help with health issues. This is the gift the Goddess gives us. Recognizing how powerful these things are is what brings the earth angel to ceremony and daily ritual.

Clearing the Space

Step into the space in which you intend to create the ceremony and sense the energies existing there. Acknowledge the air as you breathe in and exhale completely. Using the cedar as I previously described, clear the space and acknowledge the fire burning the cedar as one of five elements you are recognizing in your ceremony. Ask for the archangels to help you set your intention, aligning with the will of God and the Goddess, and hold that intention throughout the ceremony. Focus on your breathing while keeping your mind filled with the intent of surrender to the higher power. God will hear you and recognize your effort to create something beautiful on Earth.

Tools for Ceremony

Before we talk about the physical tools that an earth angel can use during a ceremony, I just want to reiterate the many personal tools earth angels have in their kit. I believe that most earth angels possess integrity, compassion, honesty, a willingness to forgive without judgment, as well as endless amounts of unconditional love. They always bring these tools to every ceremony. But along with those personal traits, I like to bring practical things into the ceremony that symbolize or evoke certain energies. I like to use tools associated with the earth and the elements: water, air, fire, earth, wood, and metal. These are all part of our natural system.

I also like to acknowledge my ancestors in all my ceremonies and put out a small plate of food as an offering. Each one of us has ancestors who watch over us and act as our guardian angels. We are always protected and guided by our loved ones who have crossed over. Honor them by acknowledging their help.

Your smudge bowl and cedar are used for clearing the space. Whether you are inside a building or outside, this will help to purify your surroundings before you begin. Have each person attending use the smoke to clear his or her energy field as well. Ask for the violet flame to cleanse and purify the space once you have gone into meditation. Archangel Michael will assist with the violet flame when you call upon him.

Your voice is a powerful tool and helps you to align your body to the frequencies of the fifth dimension. We are in a frequency where time and space shift even more than ever before by traveling on sound waves. When we use the "voice of the heart," which is true to our feelings and intention, it rises through the vocal chords and creates a powerful sound that can be released deep into the earth. Cup your hands around your mouth and create a cone of energy that goes all the way to the center of the Earth. We all express ourselves with our voice; let it be from this new vibration that we experience and express in the fifth chakra.

Your Intention

Have a bowl of water, an offering of food, and a piece of wood, metal, and earth. Put these elements in the center of the circle that you have created with your mind's eye. You can see a circle around you through your sixth chakra, or third eye, or you can actually define the circle by using a stick to carve the shape into the ground. If you are indoors, you can define your circle with fresh flowers. Begin by standing up and saying your prayer of intention, what you are doing this for, and asking God and the Goddess to hear you. Kneel down on the ground with your hands on the earth and tell her your prayer and intention. Ask that the earth's sacred energy bless your circle and carry your prayer deep into her body.

Environment for Ceremony

Ceremonies that are held out in the open, particularly in a beautiful natural environment like a forest or a park, are more powerful because we are usually closer to and more able to use the five natural elements. Plus, we can call upon the Devic kingdom for assistance when we're in natural open spaces. The reason I stress the choice of environment or space for a ceremony is because some places contain entities and spirits that we may not be aware of. I work with the archangels daily; they are the only angels I will call upon for ceremonies and rituals.

As an earth angel, I have a deep understanding of the spirit world, as well as the ability to "see" into it to know who is there and what I am dealing with. For those earth angels who do not see into the spirit world in the same way, I stress the importance of daily meditation and effort to keep the vibration high so that they can "feel" and "know" that it is only angels present and nothing more. Otherwise, entities and lower astral energies can fool you and create a presence that you might mistake as that of angels.

I worked with a woman who claims to work with angels, yet she does not see them. As with many others, she is empathic and feels everything, but without the ability to "see" as I do she was unaware that she had called entities into the space. She thought they were her helpers and spirit guides, but they were not. It is important that you keep the space in which you hold any ceremony or ritual sacred and clear. The outdoor space can be smudged just as easily as an indoor space. Holding a ceremony in an abandoned old creepy castle would not be conducive for anything other than calling in spirits that remain in a state of unrest. Often ceremonies are held in a living room at a home that has warmth and clarity in both tenant and energy. Finding a space outside that feels good and is not next to a cemetery or tragic place of the past helps to bring in a higher frequency with the earth.

Closing the Ceremony

Stand up and acknowledge the archangels for being there assisting you with your ceremony. Thank God and the Goddess for hearing your intention and prayer. Acknowledge that it is in accordance with their will that this ceremony is carried now on the wings of angels.

Ceremony, rituals, prayer, and meditation involve using and strengthening the earth angel's connection to the Divine. Without a clear and direct connection, we're not as effective in our purpose of helping others. Earth angels are defined by the energy they put out into the world, which is why I believe the process of grounding our energy, letting go of our expectations, and aligning with the Divine will keep our "spiritual telephone line" open and unencumbered.

Living at a high level of integrity, with truth, compassion, forgiveness, and love helps to nurture that connection to the Divine. Remember: we carry a particle of the Divine within our soul body and expressed through our individuality and uniqueness, which manifests through our work and mission as an earth angel.

6

Original Consciousness and Collective Karma

*Karmic events mark our journey and often
have deep emotional components that we
can spend lifetimes trying to heal.*

Original consciousness is the code in your soul body. This code, or record of your past incarnations, is directly linked to the understanding of the universe and how it works. As I have already explained, we are all carrying a particle of God within our soul body that is expressed through our individuality. Your original consciousness has detailed records of your lifetimes from all incarnations. This is also connected to the Akashic records. This great hall of information exists, according to Helena Blavatsky, the founder of the Theosophical Society, with the "indestructible tablets of the astral light" in the etheric realm. This would be the sixth realm as described in Chapter Two.

Navigating Original Consciousness for the Earth Angel

When we become an earth angel we need to tap into our original consciousness. This enables us to understand the vast amount of knowledge held by the Akashic records and accessible when helping others. Misusing this information only causes you to incur more karma. An earth angel's goal should always be to dissolve and clear karma.

An earth angel has been through many lifetimes of service, often in different cultures and as part of different religious practices, but the thread, the aspect of their lives that connects them through all lifetimes, is that of being of service to humanity. Humans have evolved in consciousness through the ages and developed a clearer understanding of their individual sensitivity. That sensitivity might be the sight of a visionary, it might be healing hands, or it might be the ability to hear guides or feel or sense what is needed. This sensitivity has also morphed into different expressions throughout the individual's history. For example, centuries ago, a person might have been a seer and through each lifetime their extraordinary gift of "sight" will have manifested or expressed in different forms, such as an astronomer, monk, midwife, farmer, slave, or cook.

There is nothing glamorous about having gifts, and people all over the world with such gifts work the fields, haul water, and scrub floors. They are earth angels who can and do help others, without revealing themselves as anything other than regular people. If we become overly inflated with the notion of being a seer or healer for lifetimes and have an attachment to that fact, we can get sidetracked and corrupt our karmic history. If we have not cleared things karmically, it will result in a trail of issues, which explains why you might be struggling with power, control, or a desire for fame and credibility.

From the beginning of time, we have worshipped and revered Goddesses and Gods, Druids and High Priestesses, all in positions of respect. As a collective, we have both honored and then demolished them because of our fear. Out of that fear came the expression of power and control that created many religions throughout history. It is from these organized platforms that humans found a way to acknowledge the existence of something more powerful than themselves, which led them to use fear to control the masses.

Even so, the spirit remains strong, and our feelings are what tell us that there is something more powerful than ourselves. We all have similar experiences through that sensitivity—fear, joy, anger, betrayal, abandonment, and many other emotional responses that have us dialed deep into our karmic history.

Understanding Karma

Earth angels meet people who, due to their karmic history, have cycles and patterns that repeat over and over. According to the *Spiritual Encyclopedia*, the definition of karma is the following:

> Karma is an ancient concept, a Sanskrit word meaning "act," "action," or "word." The law of karma teaches us that all of our thoughts, words, and actions begin a chain of cause and effect, and that we will personally experience the effects of everything we cause. We may not experience the effect (the returning karma) right away, and it may not even be in

this lifetime, but you can count on it just the same. Karma
is a cosmic law, which means that it applies to everyone,
everywhere, all the time.

In my years of working with clients and their karmic history, I
have chosen to take the meaning of karma out of the duality,
that is, the belief that doing good brings good things, doing
bad brings bad things. Instead, I use a deeper spiritual meaning of karma—its role as the unresolved emotional wounds
from our past lives. Over lifetimes, we also generate what I call
"karmic threads or emotions," such as betrayal, abandonment,
anger, belittlement, guilt, shame, and fear, which we carry
through each existence.

I believe that when we address the true karma, or vibrational match, for events in our lives, we can clear these threads
once and for all. Unresolved emotional wounds, such as the
loss of a parent as a child, being a victim of abuse, or witnessing
extreme violence in this life or past lives create karma. Karmic
events mark our journey, and often have deep emotional components that we can spend lifetimes trying to heal. Earth angels
will be able to identify more in their work by addressing their
own karma first.

I have worked with many clients who bear emotional
wounds in their present life, and many of those wounds can be
traced to their previous existences. When I am looking at past
lifetimes for a client, I will literally see the journey of their soul
going up into the ethers and back down into a lifetime, and
before my eyes the entire life is like a hologram in front of me.

I am able to trace in sequence their lives to the time they first incarnated on Earth.

I recall one example of karma in a client where the individual had been accused of being a heretic in a past life. They were sentenced to death by beheading, a common punishment during that time. As they faced death, they were of course filled with fear, felt they had been abandoned and betrayed, and experienced a wrenching separation from God. Their following incarnations, in different bodies, as different gender types, in different places around the planet, bore the same karmic theme—one of enslavement, betrayal, being wrongly accused, and often abandoned.

It is a pattern I see often, and it feeds into the collective karma. Of course, as I have previously mentioned, the unresolved issue can manifest physically. In this kind of case, I see these issues manifesting as neck pain. Medical professionals are unable to diagnose it, but as an earth angel I can help to heal this historic wound. Earth angels are called to the forefront to help people unravel the threads to their past.

Collective Karma

Collective karma is what we all share. Group experiences like war or famine leave individual emotional scars to be played out and solidified in the next life. After centuries of war and famine, we can easily see why this consciousness still exists today. We each have our own experience of that event, our individual karma, but when we engage our energy into an event we also become a part of the collective karma.

Tragic events, such as the Tohoku earthquake and tsunami in Japan in 2011, the tsunami that devastated Sumatra in 2004, or the hurricanes that changed the Gulf Coast and the East Coast forever, cause our gut to engage with sympathy with the sadness and despair of those who suffered. If we don't ground the energy into the earth, it will go out to the situation and engage with others who are also feeling the same sadness and despair. Consequently, it becomes a collective experience of sorrow, one that is repeated in the same way that individual karma cycles through life times.

Being a victim is one of the main cycles we have invested in as a collective. This pattern is something each person of every culture, gender, and religion can relate to. This manifests within the duality, and must be viewed by stepping back and observing in order to see the intricate system at play. When we carry the God particle within our bodies, have access to an infinite amount of knowledge, and incarnate allowing our physical experience to overwhelm our connection to Source, we have separation. It is through this separation that the victim role begins.

Imagine we are left by the side of the road as a baby and no one finds us until we are cold and shivering in the box in which we were abandoned. Victim? Yes, in the duality, it would be viewed that way—a helpless baby lends a victim quality to this story. However, the baby in her last lifetime may have been a man who left the mother of his child, never to have contact with them again. So karmically speaking, the baby being left on the side of the road is a continuation of the previous life, and the karmic thread is one of abandonment. More than one person is involved in this recipe for pain, which is often repeated over lifetimes, with different players taking on the roles of the person being left, the person doing the leaving, and the person watching it happen but not being able to do anything about it. Sir Walter Scott wrote, "Oh! What a tangled web we weave, when first we practice to deceive," and this would certainly express the karmic aspect of manifesting lifetimes with repeating cycles.

To understand victimization we must first look at the duality and how we invest our energy. We are constantly measuring our world through the duality, assessing whether something is right or wrong, good or bad. As a species, we have moved far away from the inner compass that naturally navigates our integrity and morality. Becoming an earth angel requires a good long look at your history and its patterns, in an effort to gain an understanding of the pain, guilt, blame, rejection, and disapproval cycles that appear regularly in your life. All human beings are victimized during their lifetimes and struggle to mend the pain they feel as a result of being separated from Source. Being of service to others means bridging the gap, and not succumbing to a belief system that you were wronged or that they did this to you.

At our best, we humans invest our energy in what is right and stand up for what we believe in. Equally, we are upset and angry about those things we know are wrong. As I explained earlier, the energy we expend is sent into these situations, so that we invest our energy there and, in turn, create more karma for ourselves and for the collective.

Does this mean we are not meant to care? No. It means that, instead, we should ground that energy—observe the right and wrong of this world but not expend energy either way. As we know, in the fifth dimension, the universe is about everything being in balance. The earth herself is constantly shifting and adjusting to maintain her balance. Through the practice of meditation, we find balance and a place of peace from which to lovingly observe rather than energetically invest in incidents or situations. We may witness tragic events, but this way we will not have an emotional charge on them.

An earth angel cannot be in service to others without this observation; otherwise, there is judgment. When we are in judgment, we are unable to see clearly beyond the situation and cannot be effectively in service to others. Judgment can be very dangerous, because it takes us out of ourselves and can transfer much deeper issues onto others or create a projection of our own fear. When we judge others, we are reacting to something within us. We judge from a deep place of fear of the unknown. Feeling out of control and afraid can bring judgment of others, causing an endless spiral of fear that in turn feeds the victimization of humanity. Judgment of any kind inevitably leads to people choosing to be a victim, which in turn locks that experience into the collective as a whole. Becoming an earth angel requires an understanding of how individual actions contribute to and solidify the collective karma.

All earth angels benefit from addressing their own victim role and delving into their patterns, especially the pattern of needing to be right or in control. We can heal family karma and collective karma by doing the work within ourselves, processing and parenting the inner child, and taking responsibility for our behavior. The path of the earth angel requires deep emotional clearing and healing. I suggest working with a teacher who will help you to move through your emotional scars, clear karma from the inside out, and help you find your place of service.

I also recommend a daily practice of forgiveness as one of the keys to healing our karma and ensuring the release of emotional attachments within the duality. As an earth angel, I am able to clear karma through a gift from my guides. I am allowed to do so because my life is dedicated to helping heal the earth and humanity.

Healing the Karmic Threads of the Past

In order to heal from the role of the victim, it helps to find times in life when you have treated another person as a victim. It might be something as simple as an experience from grade school, in which you joined with other kids laughing at or bullying another child. In fact, I believe that bullying is a long-standing collective karmic experience that has made its way into society as a defense mechanism.

Sometimes, it is difficult to admit to an incident in which we may have caused another to experience being a victim. The problem is that the ego intervenes. We do not want to acknowledge that we may have caused another to feel like a victim. "I would never do that," we tell ourselves. This is an example of resistance, in which the ego only wants to hear what it wants to hear. Our need to validate the current reality means we become masters of denial just seeking to feel good.

But earth angels understand that this is all the illusion of the duality. There is no feeling good or bad; there is just the moment we are in, and the quality of that moment is up to you. When we define our reality through the duality, we miss the opportunity to really understand why we are here. Working through the layers of the personality, ego, and karma is the pathway to our original consciousness.

A light worker called me and said she was having difficulty getting her practice going. She had such sensitivity to so many things it was hard to even function. She had studied Reiki and was ready to serve the world. The first thing I do when I work with a client is I look at their auric field. I could see she had entities around her and inside her body. I cleared them and watched as they dissolved in the light. She remarked that she felt better.

I did a process with her that introduced her inner child and allowed her to take the role of parent. Her child expressed that she felt alone. We discovered an area in her belly where she was holding some resistance about how she felt cut off from others. This stemmed from the inner child feeling separated and alone. The false ego is not something most people can see and identify, for it protects them. She was frustrated and recognized that there was a big hole in her core that related back to a time in her childhood when she was often alone, due to working parents and older siblings. She also identified her need for approval. This was directly linked to poor self-esteem. I had her and her inner child go into the core and repeat the self-esteem statement I use in my practice: *I have a right to be here as a soul in a body on the earth.* She felt this in her body and recognized she needed more tools in her tool bag.

This is a good example for upcoming earth angels to not put the cart before the horse. Take the time to learn and gather the tools you will need if you are to be in service. We gain entrance into our original consciousness by establishing self-esteem, which is built from the ground up within our core. Finding the pathway to our original consciousness is not always easy, due to the outer noise of the collective. We all embody souls that have the God particle within, and this connects all of us at the core. We share consciousness as well as earthbound karma that we have created individually and together. Understanding how to access our original consciousness is better understood by first looking at the ego.

Understanding the Role of the Ego

The ego gets a bad rap. Some people believe we should be ego-less. Part of the problem is that we rarely come across a healthy ego, so it's difficult to find healthy representations in popular culture. Television and movies have capitalized on the false ego. We see people portrayed with dysfunctional lives, yet they are glamorous and leading the way in the media. Some movies and television give more credence to beauty and how to look young than helping people deal with the reality of what life is about. The false ego provides a platform of illusion that keeps everyone engaged but not seeing what is often broken and abused within.

I find it helpful to imagine the ego as if it were a firewall around our emotional body. It keeps us safe and protected and compensates for uncomfortable feelings but, in turn, it displaces our understanding of who we really are. The firewall that is the ego detects any threat to our emotional equilibrium and will kick out unwanted truths, even though it might have been better for us to acknowledge them and act accordingly. When we stay in denial of a situation, we can continue to fool ourselves and create a bubble of belief.

Emotional wounds from childhood undermine self-esteem and damage the core self. Feelings of being wrong and not worthy of love attribute to a broken self-esteem. Ego formed from poor self-image produces a false ego, which builds around us like a house of cards. False ego sometimes displays itself as loud bravado and bold self-assurance when, in actual fact, inside the person there is a terrified inner child who learned to put forth a larger-than-life image. We spend years cultivating the ego so that we can identify who we are.

A healthy ego is strongly founded in positive self-esteem and an understanding of the core self. A healthy ego protects from a place of compassion and clarity of who we are and why we are here. When we know who we are and can be at peace with it, then our ego is healthy and supportive. Attachment to accomplishments and badges earned at school, work, socially, politically, or spiritually, feed the false ego and keep us from the truth.

The healthy ego is based on one statement: *I have a right to be here as a soul in a body on the earth.* This simple mantra is about being here without expectations and experiencing life from an authentic place that honors our right to be here. It takes a great deal of work and dedication to your path to get to a place where you are no longer attached to who you are, or what you've done, and you no longer experience separation at any level.

Being in service allows the earth angel to enjoy unlimited praise from the angels, but the work can also cause you to feel overwhelmed. When the ego has not been restructured, it is easy to feel a false sense of importance. Longing for the spotlight and competing with others can only lead to a crash-and-burn situation. Finding the balance within allows you to not be invested in the fanfare of your work, but rather detached from whatever comes up. There is a lot of hard work once you have your wings, and little to no time to bask in the sunshine of the illusion. It feels good to receive a compliment or appreciation for your work, but earth angels must remain humble in order to stay in their center, detached, and compassionate.

The Earth Angel and Original Consciousness

At first glance it appears that our karma and ego, along with the personality, prevent us from ever knowing our original consciousness. You might even ask why it seems our own body and systems work against us. Earth angels are here to show us that, in fact, they do not. Rather, it is how we have defined reality on Earth. For example, we no longer live tribally and migrate with the seasons and weather. Our technological advances have taken us away from all that is natural and earthbound. Pollution, factory farming, chemicals, and our obsession with virtual worlds mean that today we are creating a perpetual state of imbalance and losing the ability to navigate our world as we were naturally meant to.

Earth angels are here to show how to remedy this by spending time outside and connecting with the earth. The inner process each individual must face affects the balance of our planet and connecting to the earth's energies helps to keep us in personal balance. Just as we must shift and change to create harmony within the matrix of the physical, mental, emotional, and spiritual bodies, the earth shifts and changes to create balance in her body. The more we connect with the earth, the more earth angels will heed the call to serve humanity and the planet. It is the current complexity of our social structure, interwoven with technology and a fast pace, that keeps people from the simplicity of life.

We are here to feel our feelings, process them, and release them. We are the caretakers of this planet. Our experience as souls in bodies on the earth is to love at the deepest level of our being. It is that simple; yet, we look for a more complex answer. That's because we are spending so much time in the mental body, due to the fact we no longer have to hunt for our food or create a shelter to stay out of the cold. The deeper discovery that we are infinite as souls is in our original consciousness. That truth gives you the profound awareness that there is nothing for you to do but to simply be. Paradoxically, at the same time there is everything for you to do while you do nothing.

In today's society, we are defined through our egos, but back when we lived closer to the earth the only thing that mattered was survival. We were not concerned about what the other person had, for we worked together. As a tribe, we understood that it took an entire village to raise a child. We all participated in creating everything that was needed for our survival. The consciousness that is needed for today's earth angel is shared with those of the past. Many earth angels from history understood they were both nothing and everything. This can be difficult to conceptualize, if you have not yet experienced your original consciousness. This is the paradox, as I mentioned earlier, and it is best understood in this way: as people in service, we are not attached to anything; therefore, we are nothing, but we are filled with the Divine; therefore, we are everything. This profound concept is a part of our original consciousness. There is no attachment to being in service. There is no attachment to the outcome. There only is this moment and what is being felt.

Many earth angels are hearing the call to go deeper into service. They discover their part is to do the inner work and heal the emotional wounds from childhood and past lives, paving the way for others to heal as well. The ego finds balance as we take responsibility for our energy and our actions. The earth will start to heal as each person takes charge of his or her own process and creation. This level of responsibility allows us to access our original consciousness. Earth angels will recognize the need for their light to shine brightly in order for others to succeed in this journey. The planet connects everyone and is a powerful energy line that weaves us all together as one tribe.

One way to do that is through self-healing meditation.

Self-Healing Meditation

Close your eyes and find the feeling you have about another person or situation that is bothering you. Identify the feeling. Where have you created that very feeling with another? Example: You feel abandoned by your partner. Where in your past have you ever caused another person to feel abandoned by you?

Find where this is stored in your body.

Imagine yourself standing in front of you, as if you were looking into a mirror. Now reach into your body and wrap your hands around that feeling like a ball of energy, and watch it dissolve between your hands as you look yourself in the eyes and say, *I love you and I forgive you.*

Once it has dissolved, fill your body up with whatever color feels best to you, and let that color come down through the top of your head and all the way throughout your entire body.

7

Help from the Angels

We are not here to suffer but to experience
and ultimately know our true selves.

I talk to clients from all over the world about all kinds of personal issues, from health and relationships to finances and career; in fact, I think I have dealt with everything under the sun. As an earth angel, my goal is to help clients align their mental, emotional, physical, and spiritual bodies.

Before I begin any consultation, I ask that my will be in alignment with the will of God and the Goddess. This is very important, because it is not my will at work when I help a client; it is the Divine working through me as I surrender the client's illness or pain over to God and the Goddess. If I were to engage my will, believing I know what is best for that person, I would be stepping out of a much higher alignment with Source. This could end up creating more karma and causing a backlash of events on the client. Every earth angel's actions need to be accounted for, so that they are not creating more karma in this lifetime.

When I begin a session, I ask the angels to help me. I am already in a meditative state, as I see the person in their home or office and the angels accompany me as I am transported to their location. It is as if I am simply changing rooms in a house, because time and space are not really perceived in the same way. I am in my office on the West Coast of the United States, and my clients are all around the world. I am not like other people. My experience of time and space is fluid. I am able to put myself in front of someone wherever they are on the planet.

Whatever is needed in the session—physical healing, talking to loved ones on the other side, past-life karmic healing, processing the energetic emotional components out of the body—I travel with the angels and my guides and work on people just as if they were right there in front of me. Occasionally, I have a photo of the client, but most of the time I do not. I "meet" them over the phone, so all I have to go on is their voice and what I psychically see, feel, hear, and smell. With some clients, all I receive is a photo and a list of ailments—I never even talk with them; we simply communicate through email. On several occasions, I have smelled toast, stew, coffee, cigarettes, sage, and a roast cooking! I often ask the client to confirm if they have just eaten toast or smoked a cigarette.

The vision I have when I work on people is like an x-ray. I see their energy systems and work in their auric field first. The angels guide me and assist with their healing energy in all of my work. Sometimes, there is a host of angels working on the client at the same time as I am, helping me. My work as an energy surgeon requires my ability to see where the problem is and what needs to be done. If I need assistance, I ask the angels to help. They are surgeons, as well, and remove things from the body in order to heal organs, tissues, and cells.

The most important thing to remember is to surrender to their guidance. When you are working as an earth angel, trust that the archangels are there to help you and guide you, for this is key to receiving assistance. Understanding that it is not your will but God's will helps you to surrender even more. The angels' knowledge of what needs to be healed is much greater than yours. They will step in and do the work when you are beyond your abilities. This is a good reminder to allow, to let things be. We can help, heal, and comfort, but some situations are a part of a much bigger lesson for that person to be learning. We must understand that pain and illness are our teachers, some of the hardest lessons for humans. We want to feel good, and when we don't, we tap into the collective karma of "being betrayed." This betrayal takes us right back to separation, and it is imperative that humanity heals from centuries of separation.

Earth Angels at Work

SURRENDER: When we choose to step on the road to a life in service, the most important part of that journey is surrender. We surrender our lives to God and the Goddess, and we surrender our attachment to everything. Being on the path of an earth angel requires dedication, integrity, clarity, truth, and faith. Helping people to heal in the four essential bodies means being able to see, hear, smell, and feel what is happening for the individual we have chosen to work with, and receiving the guidance needed from the angels.

GUIDANCE: Each earth angel has a path that is specific to their work, and includes a wide variety of modalities. For example, the earth angel who has the gift of healing might be a massage therapist, acupuncturist, naturopath, physician, surgeon, nurse, caregiver, hospice worker, and leader of peace, energy healer, or other. The earth angel is someone who has extraordinary gifts and is appointed by the archangels to be of service.

Recognizing your gifts and following the development of those abilities with a teacher will help you become an earth angel. Guidance is always a part of every earth angel's path, whether it is from a teacher or the angels. It is important to have a strong foundation for whatever you do. A doctor goes to medical school, as does the acupuncturist and naturopath. Healers and visionaries are subject to a smorgasbord of people, workshops, and internet frenzy. Misinformation and trying to find the truth in a freeform industry can leave the earth angel-in-training a bit befuddled. Find someone whom you can trust, and stay with that teacher until you have learned all that is needed for your work. Jumping around to different classes and modalities will only confuse you and keep you questioning your own intuition. Excellent training programs that are available are listed in the back of this book.

MONEY: Healers and medicine people are criticized in some communities for receiving money for their work. But we live in modern times, and earth angels must pay their bills. Long ago, we traded for goods and services, but we cannot trade our work with the phone company. Money is part of survival, and being an earth angel means taking care of yourself so that you can help others. When receiving money for your work, let it be from a place of gratitude and awareness.

Every year, my husband and I go to visit family on the reservation. He often takes part in the traditional ceremonials, and I am responsible for preparing food and taking care of the people. When I am there, my time is totally donated to help my family and tribe. People bring me gifts, food, and their prayers. This is where I give back to the world. Not a day goes by in which I do not donate at least three hours to people in need. This is my awareness of the balance I keep within me.

WARDROBE: The earth angel is not living in biblical times, and the day of the flowing robes is gone. However, what earth angels have to offer makes us like priests and priestesses of old, so we must dress and behave as modern people do. We have to be versatile and blend in and only stand out when we need to. Being yourself and dressing to be comfortable is most important for your work and time spent helping others. You will find your authentic self is more equipped to handle your wardrobe needs than anyone else. By the time you receive your wings, you will understand that there is no need to be anything other than yourself. Like all aspects of caring for yourself, use natural products, eat organic foods, and wear natural fibers whenever possible. These are always more beneficial for the earth angel.

Working With the Archangels

I often ask the archangels to help me when I am working on someone. Archangels perform specific roles and help out in different areas of life, and are on hand to help out earth angels when they are needed. A woman called me who had dreams within dreams of alien beings manipulating her. She wanted this to stop and listed a long line of healers and shamans she had been to before me in an effort to find closure on this intrusion. She was a scientist who had huge openings in her auric field; in fact, the whole backside of her aura was missing. During our consultation, she told me that when she dreamed she saw herself asleep and dreaming in the dream. As I worked on her I saw alien beings. They were working with her while she slept. She was attached to them, believing they were helping her with her research.

I told her she must let the attachment go to avoid calling them back. I explained that I needed to repair her auric field. I closed the openings and told her that whether she knew it or not she had become dependent on them. Once I had closed all the openings in her auric field that had allowed the aliens' access to her, she experienced a peace she had not had for some time.

However, that night I woke up to find these same alien beings standing in a semi-circle around my bed. I calmly got up and went into the bathroom, sat down, and started to cry. I asked Michael, Gabriel, Raphael, and Uriel to help me. They literally took me up into the parallel universe and surrounded my body with protection. They told me not to worry, that I would always be protected. I went back into the bedroom, and the aliens were gone. I never saw them again. This is an example of how the earth angel can call upon the archangels and receive the help they need when they are in a situation that is bigger than them.

On one occasion I had been asked to work with a high-profile financial corporation in New York City. They knew about my skills as a healer and seer and brought me in as a full time consultant, advising mergers and acquisitions. This particular case resulted in my needing the assistance of Archangel Gabriel. He brings messages and helps with communication around the world and also works to clear entities.

The New York–based company was looking into a merger with another financial organization in the United Kingdom. As an earth angel, I "looked" in on meetings held by the UK organization and to my horror discovered entities in each and every member of the board. I called upon Archangel Gabriel to help me, and he came in a blaze of white light. The owner of the UK Company was in her office in England, and I was in my office in New York City. As I began my work, with the assistance of Archangel Gabriel, she stood in front of me and said, "Stop doing that! You are wrecking everything."

You can imagine my surprise that she could actually "see" me clearing people of these entities. She told me to stop. I found myself in a battle with her and her helpers—seven creepy entities that would attack me at any time of the day or night.

There was a Catholic church nearby where I would spend my lunch hour, light a candle, and pray. I was sitting on the bench across from the candles, which lined the opposite wall with rows and rows of bright lights. This area was outside, between buildings. I saw an entity jump across the buildings above, and before I could respond three shelves of candles blew off the wall, breaking all over the stone floor. I was shocked and immediately went into prayer asking Gabriel to help clear this entity from the building.

That night, the creepy seven came into my room, and I immediately called upon Gabriel, Michael, Raphael, and Uriel to help me. They battled the entities and took a hold of each one, taking them into the light. This is an important lesson to all earth angels: the understanding that it is the help of the archangels that clears this kind of astral plane activity. Clearing entities on your own can be dangerous and inappropriate. Recognizing your strengths and your humanness is important.

The physical body is often healed through the help of Archangel Raphael. Doctors, nurses, and healers call upon this benevolent being to aid and assist in healing. I always ask Raphael to help me with clients who are fighting illness, cancers, and degenerative disease.

One of my clients emailed me a photo of his mother and a list of her health concerns. She lives in Puerto Rico and was suffering from loss of appetite, scar tissue from several surgeries on her ankles and feet, insomnia, and pain throughout her body. I put on cedarwood essential oil before beginning a session. This is another form of protection that I use when I work. I instinctually knew this would be a difficult healing. I remember laughing, thinking she would probably smell it in her room in Puerto Rico! It was morning in the United States and evening in Puerto Rico, and with the help of Gabriel, who I also called upon, I cleared all kinds of entities and negative energy in her field, including one particular entity in her body, which was causing tremendous pain.

I also called upon Raphael and proceeded to clear the scar tissue out if her ankles and legs and worked on her stomach, heart, liver, pancreas, spleen, and kidneys. Her lungs needed some work, and her brain received some restructuring in the tissue. When someone is in so much pain, struggling to even get up, I will call upon Raphael to not only help me but to work on her as I work.

When I had finished with my work, I emailed her son the results. The next day he contacted me and translated his mother's email. She described that when the session began she was resting in bed and she could see a woman coming into the room smelling of a beautiful fragrance. She experienced a weight lifting from her. Afterwards, she got up and ate a light dinner, feeling hungry for the first time in months. She explained how she then went to bed and slept for 10 straight hours, waking up refreshed and with no more pain. According to her son, she has continued to live pain free ever since that session.

In this particular case, the subject was open to receiving the healing, and she was a vibrational match. Resistance prevents healing, but when someone like this woman is open, there is a chance for miraculous healing.

I call upon Archangel Uriel to assist in illuminating the truth. Uriel brings a bright gold light that fills a room and lights up all those in his presence. His sword protects. He also uses it to sever links, lifelines, and attachments.

One evening, I went to see a medium perform in a large theater with about 600 people in attendance. I sat in the balcony with a girlfriend. My husband had a seat on the main floor. Suddenly, my friend looked at me. "My head is hurting," she said. She is like the canary that gets thrown down the mine shaft to see if it's safe. Her headache immediately warned me that something was wrong. Through my psychic vision, I could see chords going out to everyone in the audience from the medium, who was still backstage preparing for the show. These chords were hooked up into the audience members' heads. By this time, my girlfriend had a full-on migraine, so I took her downstairs to some open seats where my husband was seated. When we got to him, he was also fighting a terrible headache and had reclined in his seat with his eyes closed.

I could see the deceased family members of the people who sat in the theater all talking to me, wanting a turn to be heard. In the course of three hours, the medium talked to five people, leaving many audience members disappointed that they were not picked. During the show, I could see my father and my girlfriend's uncle, both deceased, standing on the stage waving at me. They would dance around and then stop and just look at me. I asked my father, "What you are doing?" He said, "We are dancing on the stage and making all kinds of noise, and the medium doesn't see us." The medium had described a long line of spirits waiting to talk to her, and yet I did not see this line;

instead, I saw the whole theater filled with loved ones from the other side. I thanked my father because I realized everyone in the audience was having their energy sourced.

The chords hooked up to the minds of 600 people allowed her access to personal memories and details. Sourcing thoughts and memories, or hooking up chords of energy to other people, is dangerous because it is not obtaining information directly from the Divine; instead, it is receiving information against people's will. I highly recommend earth angels avoid taking shortcuts and using their gifts inappropriately. All the information you will ever require can be accessed from the Divine. In my work and throughout my life, I have never found it necessary to stray from the path of working directly with Source. It's a matter of integrity.

I immediately called upon Uriel and asked him to remove the chords. I never cut chords, links, or lifelines. as some are appropriate connections to loved ones, children, parents, and pets. I always ask Uriel to remove the inappropriate ones. These chords the medium used are invasive and can take days to recover from. Earth angels must remember that it is God and the Goddess's will, and nothing needs to be forced.

Love, Fear, and Trust

Questions about love are perhaps the most common issues I come across. For example: Why am I not loved? Why am I alone? Why did he leave me? Where is this relationship going? Central to these issues is the relationship between the individual and their inner child, and the emotional wounds left over from childhood and past lives that block us from experiencing love.

When I work with people with love issues, I take them on an inner journey to their relationship with their inner child. I teach them how to love and nurture that child the way they wanted it to be when they were younger. If there are emotional wounds, which there are in almost every case, I help them remove the energetic components of those scars from their physical body.

Through dialoguing, we will also work with their inner male and female to discover what is going on in their relationship with themselves. Past life work will reveal a loss of love or having been alone for several incarnations. I will clear these karmic events as well as address the resistance in their actual body.

In many cases, men and women have a laundry list of wants, such as career, car, money, house, and lover. They want to look a certain way and be a certain person. Usually the wants and desires are unrealistic and a bit daunting for anyone to measure up to. I teach my clients to let the laundry list go and focus on one thing: love. When we are in love, everything else falls into place. It is the natural order and balance of this world. We are not here to suffer but to experience and ultimately know our true selves.

As you experience being an earth angel, you will discover that the path of service is riddled with deep feelings. We are in service at all times, and we need to set an example to others earth angels. If you are living with dysfunction, and your life is not in balance, you need to seek out a teacher and heal within. We cannot serve others when we are ourselves are out of balance.

A woman called me about the lack of love in her life and her difficult past relationships. She wanted advice on attracting the right man. Earth angels know that all our relationships start within ourselves. If we treat ourselves with no respect, it's quite likely that we will attract someone who is disrespectful toward us. Her history showed she had an alcoholic and abusive father and a mother that was absent working all the time. She ultimately felt abandoned by her mother and betrayed by her father.

We act out all three roles throughout our lives. We are the mother, father, and the inner child at all times and in all conversations. Being aware of these different parts is one of the keys to understanding our experience here on Earth. Few people are aware enough to recognize how this triad of characters dominates our stage. We can change productions, choreograph a new show, find another director, but it will all end the same way because of our patterns, cycles, and karma. When we recognize this, heal those wounds, and change the patterns, we can achieve breakthroughs and transformation.

In this case, the client had an amazing breakthrough. Together, we processed her father's emotional abuse, which resulted in emotionally abusive adult relationships. She recognized her own participation in that cycle, having been emotionally abusive herself in other relationships and absent with her girlfriends when they needed her. After working with me and redefining her relationship with her inner child, her co-dependency, and her own alcoholic tendencies, she was able to do much deeper work and address the abuse cycles. She learned to manifest a healthy relationship. She changed the frequency of what had previously transpired to a new experience.

Of course, this does not mean she's all done. She continues to deal with the template created through the imprinting of her parents' karma and her relationship to Earth. This is something we all have to contend with throughout our lives. But by doing the inner work, we are able to manage this template and find balance. When we manage our emotions and are aware, we are able to experience the spiritual and, in turn, bring balance into the physical.

It often seems that we blame our parents for all our troubles. But there are no faults. Parents are the children of other parents, and so the cycle goes on and on. We often end up parenting without any guidance or help. There's no manual available to helps us parent. In the same way, there is no manual to teach us at 18 years old how to parent our inner child. We must rely on our courage and inner guidance. The earth angel has the opportunity to set the stage, doing the inner work and, by example, parenting their own inner child. This inadvertently helps the people around them, even if they are not ready. As more and more earth angels gather to be in service, the consciousness starts to shift, helping people to tackle their biggest fears.

Let's look at another example.

A client called me with chronic fear—fear of driving, fear of what would be on the road, fear of what would be there when she arrived, and fear of life itself. I found that her fear was something she had experienced as an infant. She was being molested by her brothers, and her father caught them and placed her in the family car and drove away angry and scared. All of these experiences locked her into a cycle of fear. This cycle is constant in her daily life, from her own fear to what lies around the next corner. I wanted to know what she did to manage the fear and discovered that she had gone through extensive therapy and used medication. This kind of information is valuable to earth angels working at this level.

This woman had experienced emotional arrest because of the molestations, and her life was severely damaged. I knew I needed to treat her with the upmost care. Together, we processed the inner child and found a core wound and a place to start the healing work. I removed the energetic emotional components from her body, and she began to feel relief and to breathe easier. We released the fear and moved her into a higher vibration. Two weeks later, she was driving and feeling comfortable and confident behind the wheel. She was amazed.

When earth angels are in service, they deal with all kinds of people with all kinds of personal issues. Not surprisingly, the issues that come up are ones that the earth angel is dealing with, and they are present in the collective. In cases like this, earth angels need to take care not to enmesh with the client. Draw clear boundaries as to your issues and those of the client. Earth angels that have done extensive inner work are more able to step back and observe where another person is coming from.

In the work of an earth angel, you might find others projecting their insecurities and fears onto you. Their lack of trust within themselves will want to test you. This testing is about their insecurity and not trusting their own intuition. Help the client to uncover where they are in resistance to trusting others and ultimately themselves. You will find many people going into transference speaking to you as if you were their mother or father, unaware that they are transferring these roles onto you. Your boundaries must be clear, and the ability to see that this is taking place will help you to better identify their needs. We can speak gently, and with guidance help others to find their resistance. This also applies to helping people with the process of death and dying.

One day a man called me from the hospital and told me that his mother was dying of stage four cancer of the stomach. He wanted me to talk to her and help her transition. His voice was weak. He was scared. I told him I could see his own mother's parents standing on either side of the bed. They were waiting for her. She was happy they were there. I told him that I also saw the Virgin Mary. The mother had been praying to the Virgin Mary and asking for her help. The prayers had been answered: the Virgin Mary was there to guide the mother as she passed over. Her son called me later that night and told me she had died, and I felt so honored to have been a part of her transition.

This experience is a perfect example of the responsibility earth angels bear for communicating clearly with the spirit universe. Sometimes when people "see" things, they don't understand whether they are seeing angels or entities. This is because their clairvoyance is not fully developed. Other people who do not have visions rely on their feelings. Still others only hear angels and do not see them. Proper training with a teacher and dedication to a meditation practice all help the earth angel to develop their gifts and utilize them appropriately. Unfortunately, earth angels have to be prepared to go through the fires of transformation and recognize that karma always plays a part in the development of the earth angel's abilities.

Conscious Practice for the Earth Angel

Meditation is the foundation for all earth angels. Creating a platform of peace allows the earth angel to discern while helping others. Keeping your meditation going while you are walking, talking, and moving through your day is important to maintaining a higher frequency.

We can raise our vibration by closing our eyes and seeing ourselves holding ourselves as a newborn baby. Allow your heart to open and fill the baby up with love. See the baby's heart open and fill you up with love. Now see yourself standing in front of you, loving the picture of you loving the baby and the baby loving you. This is done slowly, with your breath filling your lungs and exhaling completely. We can continue to see ourselves over and over, loving this picture and expanding our auric field. This raises the frequencies and keeps your energy protected.

Another useful practice is reweaving the etheric web, which surrounds your auric field about six feet out from your body. All it takes is your focus and putting your mind on it. Simply say in your mind: *I am now reweaving my etheric web.* This is done automatically, and if you notice any holes or tears you can use a gold or silver thread to repair it. This is also a great protection for the energy field.

Asking the Divine for the blue light of protection will also keep you safe when you are working on others. If you are a healer, make sure you put blue light gloves on and shield your wrists, elbows, and shoulders with protection. After you have worked on a client, always wash your hands with cold water. Use cedar to smudge and clear your auric field each time you work. If you do not clear yourself, you are collecting other people's energy on your hands, arms, and without shields right into your body. If you work on someone who has cancer or a disease, this is dangerous. Earth angels must be responsible and protect themselves.

When as an earth angel you feel ready, you can ask the archangels to help you to be in the appropriate realm. You may feel the energy increase as you shift into the fourth realm. You can remain there during the course of the healing. You might experience coming back into the third realm and recognize you have shifted. This is common, and each time you meditate you can ask to go back into the fourth realm with the help of the archangels. This is based upon your development and what is right for you at this time, with practice and meditation daily.

Each earth angel is responsible for what they do with their energy and gifts. Remember when we cross over we are not asked about the badges we earned and how much money we made; we are asked how much did we love and did we love those people around the world as much as we loved our children, mother, father, sisters, and brothers? The earth angel loves everyone unconditionally.

8

Finding Your Wings

The experience of the Divine can be as
simple as closing your eyes in meditation.

Our busy 21st-century schedules and modern environ-ment constantly challenge us, impacting both our health and energy and leaving earth angels feeling depleted and tired. I know how important it is to take care of ourselves inside and out so that we can effectively do our work. Here are some of my suggestions for doing precisely that.

Diet

Earth angels will find a diet rich in organic fruits and vegeta-bles and free of chemicals and pesticides most supportive of their energy. Of course, this means shopping for organic food and avoiding any thing processed. I also supplement my diet with vitamins, and I am a big fan of Juice Plus, which consists of 100-percent freeze-dried organic fruits and vegetables in gel caps. This product is sold nationwide and offers distribution programs. I find them a great way to meet my daily require-ment of phytonutrients and keep the immune system boosted.

Some dieticians and doctors suggest going by your blood type when designing a diet to suit you. Dr. Peter J. D'Adamo, the author of *Eat Right 4 Your Type,* provides a guide to your specific blood type that helps to clarify sensitivity to certain foods, allergies and chronic illness. The book also helps to distinguish which earth angels require animal proteins and which do not.

Overall awareness of what you eat moves into a vibrational category as you hone your skills. The earth angel who is working as a healer can feel this intensify as their energy becomes more attuned. Some foods become near impossible to eat because the frequency does not match your own. Earth angels should stay away from alcohol, since it depletes energy and adds pollutants to their sensory filters. When energy drops, openings in the auric field appear, allowing lower astral plane entities into the space.

The foods and beverages we consume feed our body on a cellular level. I highly recommend asking for the violet flame to clear your food and asking for the white light and angels to bless your meal. When we enter into conscious eating, we start to feel what the food does for our body and how it affects our mood. Earth angels must be careful to not eat erratically and cause food-induced emotional reactions. The highs and lows experienced by our nourishment can cause the scale to tip in the natural balance of the yin and the yang.

In the *Book of Oriental Diagnosis* by Muchio Kushi, he explains this. Too much salt, meat, eggs, and cheese are the extremes of yang foods that can cause contraction, condensation, anger, and upset in the gentlest of people. Too much sugar, alcohol, and drugs are the very extreme yin energy that causes expansion, differentiation, and outward expression. Balancing yin and yang energy requires recognizing what food feels like in your body; meat may pull you out of balance in one direction while sugar may pull it in another. Earth angels are looking to stay in the middle, and fruits and vegetables are the best way to do that.

Drugs

Among my clients are people who say they are healers or intuitives, and yet they admit to me that they smoke pot on a regular basis. Of course, it is no surprise to me to find all sorts of entities and holes in their auras when I begin working with them because marijuana use prevents them from effectively blocking negativity. I advise them to stop using marijuana if they want to stay safe and be effective.

A popular ceremony that people have traveled to South America for is the ayahuasca ceremony. People have reported receiving tremendous insight about themselves, the earth, and the universe. Ceremonies like this use a variety of plants prepared with *banisteropsis caapi* vine, a potent hallucinogenic. I do not recommend taking part in a ceremony like this unless there is real guidance.

A true shaman is as hard to find as a true psychic. We forget that some people want power, and through these ceremonies they try to achieve it. Corruption and anger can be the downfall of some of the most highly gifted people. Some ceremonies practiced by indigenous cultures are incredibly powerful, and some people have ill intentions. Black magic might be aimed at an innocent foreigner. I have cleared many clients who have come home from this ceremony, unaware of the misuse of power. Ceremonies are very important all over the world, but always take care to find out who is running the ceremony and then ask why you need to be there. The experience of the Divine can be as simple as closing your eyes in meditation. We only look for the wow factor in ceremonies like this because we have lost our trust and feel separate from the Divine.

Ultimately, smoking pot and using alcohol or prescription medications to get to an altered state of consciousness lower an earth angel's frequency and leave them open to harmful energy. Earth angels gain greater knowledge and finesse their skills through the steady practice of meditation with the guidance of a teacher who is there to follow up with questions and help with their inner development. Yes, that long road to one's enlightenment always circles back around to sitting in silence. Your connection with the Divine is greatly enhanced through the vibration you put in your body.

Earth Medicine

There are cultures around the world with shamans and witch doctors that practice different forms of earth medicine. While most of them are legitimate, there are many others, particularly on popular tourist routes, who have deviated from the path, thereby corrupting their gifts and hurting people to gain power and control.

I experience much of the world's population operating from the third chakra, or power center, and not connecting to the magnitude of the heart. Feeling unacknowledged can keep many people locked into old patterns of behavior. This is why being an earth angel is an appointed position from the archangels. There are many self-appointed shamans and gurus who have not done the due diligence to bear such a title. The collective wound of separation from Source is what creates the need for self-importance and yearning for recognition from others. This goes back to the false ego and how we need to rebuild a healthy core of self-esteem. People search for the wow moment in their spiritual evolution, wanting to see the spirits or hear them, and often miss the signs given to us by Source.

I had a client call me and tell me she had had cancer four times in the last 10 years. We discussed her illness and how she was terrorized at night by spirits. I kept asking her, "Have you traveled anywhere?" Lo and behold, in the last 15 minutes of the session, she said, "Oh, I forgot to tell you: 10 years ago, I went to South America to study with a shaman with a group of Austrians." Bingo! There was the reason she had gotten so ill and continued to manifest cancer throughout her body.

Through remote viewing, I went to the area the shaman was in, and I could see the black magic he had created to harm her and the Austrians. His ill intent to hurt them was due to his perception. His jealousy and anger were pointed at their wealth, their ability to travel, and his perception that they were there to take his sacred ways. I cleared all kinds of entities and energies used against the woman and her travelling companions. She reported weeks later that her cancer was in remission and she was no longer feeling terrorized at night. This is a good example of why we must be careful about whom we go to for help and what we are seeking.

There are good teachers who will care for your safety and well-being, and there are emotionally wounded, angry people who are not ready to be guides. I hear a lot of stories from people seeking a spiritual path who are searching for the right teacher. Sometimes, our karmic history is like a beacon for manifesting what we need ultimately to heal. We find ourselves drawn to certain cultures through a connection we feel that can bring forth the right teacher. What we experience in that pursuit might also be the energy that went unresolved in our past.

The dynamics between student and teacher must be ones of mutual trust, with the teacher being able to see what the karmic connection is and caring for that student with regards to the shared history. It's important to be discerning and to make sure your teacher has achieved a state of consciousness that allows for them to be in that role.

Boundaries

Earth angels need to be very clear about their boundaries. Setting healthy boundaries requires a sound definition of the core self—in other words, knowing who we are. The core self is home to self-esteem derived from those formative years between the mother's womb and the age of three. During these early years, we imprint our parents' behavior woven with karma. Once the incredible orchestration of the template is built, the stage is set for the cycles to run. These cycles consist of emotional wounds, a series of feelings created from a specific event. It is possible to have our boundaries breached when these cycles are in play, because those overwhelming feelings are triggered and felt again right down to the original wound. Once again the earth angel's job is to first identify the cycles and manage those boundaries.

For example.

A client tells me the story of how her mother was never home and she was left to care for her younger siblings. Her father left when she was two years old. The feelings in this cycle are best described as responsibility, denial, worry, anger, betrayal, abandonment, and loneliness. As we talk, I can see that she has translated this through her life by taking on responsibility for others, staying in denial of the dysfunction, becoming worried for her own safety, angry that she feels trapped, betrayed by the partner who has now left her, abandoned by God, and ultimately alone. This pattern wheel can reoccur throughout her life until she sees the repetition and addresses the emotional components within.

When she values who she is at the core with the self-esteem definition, *I have a right to be here as a soul in a body on the earth*, she is able to set the boundaries of her work, not take on other people's energy or illnesses and respect herself. It is important for her to learn to say no and stand by that and recognize where she steps into the little girl role to better manage a situation that feels all too familiar.

This kind of recognition is critical for all earth angels and their work. The boundary of being the parent and guiding the inner child is the biggest hurdle for an earth angel. Being a healer means knowing what your limits are and expressing your boundaries clearly. When another person wants you to play a part in their pattern wheel, you can recognize this and remain the observer. Another earmark of healthy boundaries is having compassion and love for the world but a strong guidance from your inner compass that will navigate you beyond the duality.

Co-dependency

Earth angels need to be watchful of co-dependency, since this is a frequent issue in our families of origin. This is a popular term and covers different ground, including being in relationship with someone who is addicted to alcohol or drugs, caretaking, or enmeshing with others. Melody Beattie, the author of *Codependent No More*, defines co-dependency as: "A codependent person is one who has let another person's behavior affect him or her, and who is obsessed with controlling that person's behavior." In my observation, co-dependency is not only traced through the family of origin but is a sociological problem.

Earth angels need to be aware of their own history as well as able to identify what a client is going through. I had a client call me and proudly announce she had ended her relationship with her alcoholic boyfriend. She was moving on to a brighter future. This woman's voice had raised 10 octaves, and she sounded like a little girl. I could hear the fear and the inner child and recognized she was in a cycle that had her headed straight for another destructive relationship. The voice of the little girl was trying to convince me that everything was okay and that she was ready to find the love of her life. I could hear that she felt out of control and was fearful, for she no longer had someone to blame and be the victim of.

I intercepted and did some processing with her inner five-year-old and discovered the energetic emotional components that were lodged in her physical body that were triggering the old pattern and wounds of fear, betrayal, abandonment, and shame. Her inner child got to tell her parents how she felt about being afraid, alone, and ashamed of things that as a five-year-old she had no control over. She also got to tell them that as a five-year-old, she did not need the responsibility of acting like an adult; she just wanted to play. She released this and made room for a higher frequency that I brought down into her body, filling up all the spaces that were cleared.

In a world where people are constantly vying for power and control over one another, the victim role often gets played by the benevolent and kind-hearted co-dependent. They say yes when they mean no. Others co-dependents are riddled with guilty feelings and often leave this earth believing they did not do enough.

Being codependent does not mean you are defective or inferior. The behavior usually comes from the necessity to protect our self and meet our needs. Earth angels need to identify any co-dependent patterns in themselves, so that they can better serve others. Some classic signs of co-dependent behavior are: feeling responsible for others, their feelings, actions, choices, wants, needs, well-being, lack of well-being, and ultimate destiny, along with the fear of rejection, taking things personally, guilt and shame, controlling, anxiety, low self-esteem, and a tendency to ignore problems, overeat, wonder why they feel like they are going crazy, and not feeling happy, content, or peaceful with themselves.

How do we identify patterns? Earth angels learn to listen in a unique way. It is as if the words you hear from the client are suspended in the air in front of you. You start to hear patterns in what the client is talking about. As you refine your gifts, you will learn to identify feelings that tell you what needs to be addressed. I find it important to take my time and not rush ahead with telling my client what I perceive. Instead, I allow for a natural process where the client can discover their own resistance for themselves. Self-discovery is always more powerful than anything we earth angels can say or do. An earth angel guides and assists where they are needed.

Conscious Practice for the Earth Angel

A PRAYER FOR THE EARTH ANGEL: Thank you for my life God and the Goddess! I am here to serve with humility, respect, and integrity. I am grateful for the help I receive from the archangels and ask that they assist me in all that I do. I surrender my life to service and ask that my will be in alignment with the will of God and the Goddess, for the highest good of everyone and the highest good of the universe.

DAILY INNER CHILD CONNECTION: Close your eyes and see yourself as a child crawling or walking up to you. Pick them up and ask them how they are feeling. Feel your heart opening up and filling them up with love and their heart filling you up with love. Tell them you are parenting them now. You can see how bright, beautiful, talented, creative, and sensitive they are. Put your hand on the child's heart and affirm they have a right to be here as a soul in a body on the earth. Give the child a hug and a toy to play with and send him or her off to play.

CORE SELF-ESTEEM BUILDING: Close your eyes and ask your inner child to go with you to the core of your being. This core lies between the heart and the solar plexus. Both of you place your hands on the core and say, *I have a right to be here as a soul in a body on the earth.* Let that translate through your hands into the core of your being. Let the child say it again. Feel what the core looks like and the changes that take place. Return each day to do this until your core is filled with this vibration.

MEDITATION FOR YOUR INNER LIGHT: Close your eyes and feel roots like a tree growing off your body. Ground them deep into the earth. Feel earth energy rise up the roots filling your body. Feel your heart like a three-dimensional sun, with rays of love shining inward and shining outward. Go into the core of your being, where your self-esteem lives. See the light that shines bright from this center. Let this light grow and become brighter and brighter, filling up your whole body. Let the light expand farther and fill your auric field. Let this light continue into the universe and connect with the Divine. This is the God particle within you connecting with Source.

MEDITATION WITH THE ARCHANGELS: Close your eyes and ground your energy deep into the earth. Ask the archangels to surround you. Ask them to cleanse and purify your auric field and body with the violet flame. Ask them to give you guidance on your path and help you to be the best you can be, with your will aligned with Source. Ask the angels to guide you and show you the way. If there is a message you need to receive ask for that message now. Tell the angels you are grateful for all of their help.

These meditations and prayers will help earth angels to be in a state of service. This path is difficult with challenges at every turn. Let your faith carry you and your intention be true.

Conclusion

Becoming an earth angel is like a dance choreographed by the Divine, and I have written this book to welcome you to the dance. I honor and appreciate all those who feel the calling to help others and surrender to a life of nonattachment and inner peace. You will discover, as I have, that living a life of purpose is both challenging and rewarding. I hope that I have also shown you that when you are filled with your own approval and self-love you are more able to give unconditionally to others. Earth angels are authentic and act with integrity and humility. This above all sets them apart from other light workers. The statement and unquestionable truth that *we have a right to be here as a soul in a body on the earth* provides a solid and unshakeable foundation and is what steers our purpose and helps to navigate our service, providing healing, compassion, and radiant love.

We are living through a special time, which brings many difficulties and problems to the fore, as well as opportunities for all life on this planet. After many lifetimes on Earth spent in the fourth dimension, this new higher frequency, the fifth dimension, has created the right atmosphere and conditions for a new order of earth angels. It also requires all humans to adjust to this higher vibration, which is related to the fifth chakra in the body. I have explained how the fifth dimension opens up a whole new experience for humanity, with many people feeling vulnerable and spiritually motivated to reconnect with their original consciousness. Consequently, earth angels will come across more seekers and people looking for guidance than ever before.

I have also shown the complexity of this new dimension. As earth angels develop, they will begin to understand that within the fifth dimension, there are openings to other dimensions, a gateway to other realities that the earth angels will help to integrate with a host of galactic travelers. Before long, I believe that earth angels will realize that it is a multidimensional reality and one that they will gain a better understanding of through a daily practice of meditation.

A daily ritual of meditation is one of my key recommendations to earth angels, because it helps to strengthen and refine our connections. As well as a special connection to the angels, who we call upon and work with every day, earth angels also have a singular connection to the Divine. This is their greatest strength and must be nurtured through prayer and meditation. As effective earth angels, we must be able to step back and observe what others are going through without engaging our own desire to change, fix, or rescue. In other words, it is about living outside of the duality, where we can view life through the lens of peace. It is always God and the Goddess' will, not ours.

I have also offered my understanding of the archangels, developed over 30 years of work as an earth angel, upon whom we can call at any time. While other teachers write about their angel experiences, I have focused on archangels Gabriel, Michael, Uriel, and Raphael, because these are the angels I work with. When working with the archangels, it is important to remember that they are always there whenever you need them.

While I have focused a lot of my attention on the process and development of becoming an earth angel, I have also gone into a lot of depth about how to handle and what to expect from the people you might come across in your work. For example, I have shared a lot of my knowledge about karma, both individual and collective, about past lives and how to clear them, and about the original consciousness. However, it is my experience that being separated from Source is perhaps the central issue human beings face and the most important reason why earth angels are needed even more so today.

When we incarnate we are unable to remember our past lives, because we are so overwhelmed with the dense human form we have embodied, which results in amnesia and forgetting why we are here and what we are meant to do. We are struggling as a species, rushing headlong to the finish line when everything that we are seeking has always been with us. By feeling our feelings, we experience the energy that links us back to Source. I urge everyone to reconnect with the earth, in such a way that they can experience the earth's energy coming up through the feet and the divine energy descending through the top of the head, creating a fusion of energy in the heart that is the expression of divinity in physical form.

As an earth angel, I am challenged each day with every kind of story, problem, and health issue, and with working one person at a time to clear the resistance and help people find their inner freedom. Ultimately, the road to understanding and reconnecting to Source leads us to the heart. I believe in the power of love, and as an earth angel, I try to share my love each and every moment with a prayer or thought for someone who is suffering and in pain. I am sending that powerful love that is created from divine alchemy in the heart to those who are in need. Sometimes I even find myself clearing congested energy off the guy who works on my car while I sit and wait, or the text message that comes in from a friend who is suffering with the news of cancer. I send out this love, because it is the most powerful energy known to all humanity.

Over three decades, I have devoted my life to the Divine and our beautiful earth, and my purpose has been to care for people wherever they are in the world. I have seen the similarities we all share with our emotional body and our disconnection from Source. I was appointed by the archangels to do my work, and they have guided me in writing this book. Earth angels are called to Earth at this time. I encourage you to dedicate yourself to the Divine through humility, compassion, sensitivity, and most of all love. It is through this devotion and daily practice that you too can receive your wings.

About Sonja Grace

For over 30 years, author and mystic healer Sonja Grace has been offering her clients, both in the United States and abroad, immediate stability, clarity, and guidance. Through her healing, counseling, and spiritual processing, Sonja has a wide variety of talent to choose from in which she accesses her ability to channel and communicate with the Divine. She sees and receives messages from loved ones who have crossed over and offers a venue for healing in this world and the spirit world. Her ability to read and clear the karmic threads to past lives helps clients heal lifetimes of patterns.

Sonja is an energy surgeon and helps clients to identify where the discomfort is in the physical, emotional, mental, or spiritual bodies. She provides medical scans and defies time and space with her energy medicine, etheric clearing, structural and cellular healing work, and helping the client to transform their energy, chakras, auric field, as well as the physical body in all systems. Sonja is able to execute all levels of her work from a distance and over the phone. Her education includes Neuro Linguistic Programming, Trager therapy, Feldenkrais, Polarity, Energy Medicine, Touch for Health, Energy work, Etheric work, and Deep Processing with the inner child. Sonja also shares her years of dance training through different forms of movement therapy that includes micro movement and yoga. She teaches meditation, workshops, retreats, and training courses. Sonja lives with her husband in Portland, Oregon.

Bibliography

BEATTIE, MELODY. *Codependent No More*. Hazelden Foundation, 1986.

BRENNEN, BARBARA. *Light Emerging*. Bantam Books, 1993.

GALLAGHER, JAMES. "Global cancer cases reach 14 million, World Health Organization says." BBC News. December 12, 2013

KUSHI, MUCHIO. *Book of Oriental Diagnosis*. Japan Publications, Inc., 1980.

WATERS, FRANK. *Book of the Hopi*. Penguin Books, 1977.

FACTS FROM WATER.ORG *http://water.org/water-crisis/water-facts/water/*

Resources

The Barbara Brennan School of Healing,
www.barbarabrennan.com

Eden Energy Medicine,
www.innersource.net

Energy Medicine: The Subtle Body,
www.cyndidale.com

ECH Training,
www.sonjagrace.com

FINDHORN PRESS

Life-Changing Books

Consult our catalogue online
(with secure order facility) on
www.findhornpress.com

For information on the Findhorn Foundation:
www.findhorn.org